Pearls for Eternal Life

Study Guide that Leads You on the Eternal Way

Sharon Elizabeth De Jager

WORKBOOK PRESS LLC
187 E Warm Springs Rd,
Suite B285, Las Vegas, NV 89119, USA

Website: https://workbookpress.com/
Hotline: 1-888-818-4856
Email: admin@workbookpress.com

Ordering Information:
Quantity sales. Special discounts are available on quantity purchases by corporations, associations, and others.
For details, contact the publisher at the address above.

Library of Congress Control Number:
ISBN-13:   978-1-957618-93-7 (Paperback Version)
                              (Digital Version)

REV. DATE: 04/03/2022

Pearls for Eternity

A Study Guide to lead you on the path of Eternity

Jesus said:
"Do not accumulate for yourselves treasures on earth,
where moth and rust destroy and
where thieves break in and steal.
But accumulate for yourselves treasures in heaven,
where moth and rust do not destroy, and
thieves do not break in and steal.
For where your treasure is,
there your heart will be also."
Matthew 6:19-21

Sharon E De Jager

INDEX

A WORD FROM THE AUTHOR

Dear Reader

Pearls are formed through a painful process within the mussel's shell and its flesh. The pearl is formed due to a painful irritation of a grain of sand which is caught up in this very spot of the mussel. It secretes a flued to try and get rid of the grain of sand which is not successful. The pearl grows and can cause the death of the mussel while producing a very precious jewel.

The narratives and writings in this book, is the result of different painful experiences which our Heavenly Father allowed to form many different spiritual pearls. These precious spiritual pearls have enriched my spiritual life and resulted in the removal of many things and characteristics in my life which did not glorify God.

A few years passed by in which God progressively made me understand that these spiritual pearls have become a belt around my waist and many strings of pearls are hanging from it. It was my responsibility to share these pearls with others as the Holy Spirit leads me, but it was important to be sensitive and have discernment with whom I share these precious pearls so that they are not thrown to the pigs where they will be trampled upon as Jesus said in Matthew 7:6.

As time moved on the writing of this book was born within my heart to exclusively glorify God. An urgency to let this book see the light followed under inspiration of our Heavenly Father.

Yet the Word came from Him: "My Word is truth. There is no greater truth than this! I am the Alpha and Omega of all truth. My truth leads to eternal life. Follow Me and you will live. Live in the truth that I give. I am the Way, the Truth, and the Life. I have come that you may have life and have it abundantly." Therefore, the pearls are fastened to a Girdle around your waist — the Belt of Truth.

No matter what I would write, even if, according to my conviction, that it would be Holy Spirit inspired, it can never be considered higher than the Word of God, namely, the Bible! May every person reading these writings be impeded to take up the Word of God himself and measure the writings to them. The Bible is the most exalted Truth of all time, and my writings are subordinate and in the shadow of God's all-conquering Word and Truth. It should never be viewed differently, for God alone has the final say on everything in, above, below, and around this world.

It is my deepest longing and desire that He alone be glorified in and through these writings and that His Kingdom will be expanded through them; that everyone reading this will come to a deeper relationship and experience with the King of all kings.

May you embark on the life-enriching journey of discovery and find various spiritual pearls that will contribute to the treasures you accumulate in heaven as described in Matthew 6:19-21 and at the same time experience a life-enriching experience in God's presence.

- Sharon E De Jager -

ACKNOWLEDGEMENTS

First, above all and all, I want to thank my Heavenly Abba Father who inspired and moved me by His Spirit to write down everything He has revealed to me in so many precious ways. He satisfied my enduring spiritual hunger and thirst with heavenly abundance and still does. He is and remains the Alpha and Omega of my existence, the all-encompassing Love that has become the heartbeat of my life. Without Him I am nothing, in Him I have found fulfillment!

I want to thank my husband, Rudi, for his constant loving encouragement, prayers, and support to motivate me to make this book come to light. I thank our Heavenly Father who, in His wisdom had ordained that the two of us could find each other in true love. It is amid this love that a once lost and deeply buried God-given talent has come back to the surface, to emerge in this way. Rudi, thank you for allowing Abba Father to use you to see my life again in new, colorful perspective. A perspective that led to a richer relationship in Him.

I would also like to thank Pastor Bert Murray who allowed God to convey His mysteries to him and that he would make them known to us again so that we too could receive deeper insights. Thank you for the encouragement to convey these truths to a spiritually needy humanity as well.

The God-given influence of my parents, who in obedience to our Heavenly Father, has guided me in the ways of the Lord and instilled in me the seriousness of an active, growing relationship with the Lord, cannot be minimized either. I thank our Heavenly Father for the spiritual foundation and love they have built into my life.

I would also like to thank everyone who has had a profound impact on my life and who have been instrumental in the hands of our Heavenly Father to shape my life according to His will. Some of you don't even realize it.

- *Sharon E De Jager* -

ACKNOWLEDGEMENT

Scriptures are quoted from the Bible,
the New & Old King James Versions,
the New English Translation,
and the Amplified Bible.

The writings in this book
are directed to
All who desire to know God in depth,
through a deeper relationship and
experience with Him.
Longing to hear one day:
"Come, you blessed of My Father,
Inherit the kingdom that was prepared for you
from the foundation of the world."
Matthew 25:34

I. *THE MOST IMPORTANT INVITATION OF ALL TIME*

Revelations 3:18,20

Jesus said:" Take My advice
and buy gold from Me, refined by fire
so you can become rich!
Buy from Me white clothing
so you can be clothed and
your shameful nakedness will not be exposed, and
buy eye salve to put on your eyes
so you can see!
Listen! I am standing at the door and knocking!
If anyone hears my voice and opens the door
I will come into his him and
share a meal with him, and he with Me."

HAVE YOU EVER PURCHASED ANYTHING FROM JESUS?

Revelation 3:14-18
"To the angel of the church in Laodicea write the following:
"This is the solemn pronouncement of the Amen,
the faithful and true Witness,
the Originator of God's creation:
'I know your deeds, that you are neither cold nor hot.
I wish you were either cold or hot!
So because you are lukewarm, and neither hot nor cold,
I am going to vomit you out of My mouth!
Because you say,
"I am rich and have acquired great wealth, and need nothing,"
but do not realize that you are wretched, pitiful, poor, blind, and naked,
take My advice
and buy gold from Me refined by fire
so you can become rich!
Buy from Me white clothing so you can be clothed and
your shameful nakedness will not be exposed, and
buy eye salve to put on your eyes
so you can see!"

John, an apostle of Jesus Christ, revealed the revelation of Jesus Christ, as God had given Him to show His servants what was about to happen. As from Revelation 1, John, among other things, also reveals messages to seven congregations that existed in Asia at that time.

Each congregation had their own "spiritual character" that included good and bad points. John was to write these messages in letters to each congregation as Jesus Christ gave him the messages. Here we see Jesus addressing the leader/pastor of each congregation as the "angel of the congregation." In Hebrews 1:7& verse 14, we see that angels are not only serving spirits but are also defined as messengers of God. The example of each congregation and the messages given to each of these seven congregations by Jesus, were not only applicable for that time, but also applicable for the modern church of today. It still has deep value today for everyone who opens his or her heart to allow the voice of Jesus to be heard in their lives.

I want to draw your attention to the congregation of **Laodicea.**

Laodicea was a rich city in Asia where Paul also preached the Gospel and established a congregation. Laodicea was known for their beautiful black wool clothing which they wedged and sold. They were also known for the special eye salvage/ointment they made, which they believed could prevent blindness. However, the city of Laodicea had one problem that also led to the downfall of the city in later years. They did not have any fresh water. The water was of volcanic origin, with many impurities in it and was always lukewarm, tasted bad and made people nauseous and sick with a stomach disorder. They had to get fresh water with a pipe plant from a nearby town.

Here in Revelation, we see that Jesus, through John, conveys a message to this congregation. The message is as follows:

This congregation of Laodicea was under the wrong impression. They were under the impression that they are rich, well clothed, that they have good eyesight, and have great understanding in all things. They worshipped God with a false heart out of obligation. Their motives toward God were not pure and a love relation with Him was lacking. Wealth dulled their need for God, and they lived for themselves, reaching out no hand to the needy. They fell back again in their old pattern of sin, some in secret, others openly. Yet they believed that the ritual of going to church was enough. They assumed that they are perfect. This congregation thought they were on the main road to heaven!!

But Jesus said that they are <u>poor, blind, and naked</u>! Moreover, they are <u>like the lukewarm waters</u> of their city! See Revelation 3:15-17.

This statement or message is also meant for us today. We live in a time when Jesus is no longer a priority in most people's lives and symbolically speaking, many of us are in the same circumstances as this congregation. One of the greatest obstacles that many children of the Lord live with, is that they do not see the need to spend quality time with God's Word, the Bible, through which they can build their relationship with Him.

The congregation of that time no longer exists, but his message in view of what Jesus said, is still alive today, confronting each of us with the following questions...
- What does our spiritual life and relationship with the Lord look like?
- Is our relationship hot, lukewarm, or ice cold??
- Are we in a living, growing relationship with the Lord, clothed in His white robes, with gold in our hearts and ointment for our eyes??

Jesus warns the people, but also gives the best "prescription" for the problem.
Look at **Revelation 3:18** once again: -
"Take My advice and buy gold from Me, refined by fire so you can become rich!
Buy from Me white clothing so you can be clothed, and your shameful nakedness will not be exposed, and buy eye salve to put on your eyes so you can see!"

What does Jesus mean when He tells us
to buy these goods from Him?
What and how can you and I buy from Jesus?
Let us find the answers further in His Word...

WHAT DOES "GOLD REFINED BY FIRE" REPRESENT?

Revelation 3:18
Jesus said: "Take My advice and <u>buy gold from Me, refined by fire so you can become rich!</u> Buy from Me white clothing so you can be clothed, and your shameful nakedness will not be exposed, and buy eye salve to put on your eyes so you can see!"

Malachi 3:2b-3 gives us the answer to the phrase "gold refined by fire." Our hearts are very precious to the Lord, so precious that He compares them to the qualities of gold and silver. Here the Lord says He is the goldsmith who sits ready to evaluate and purify our hearts.

When gold is extracted from the rock, it is impure and unusable, but when it passes through the fire, it is purified. Impure gold is hard and partly adopts the properties of what it is mixed with. It's called an alloy. Pure gold is soft, flexible, rusty, does not easily lose its luster. The purer the gold, the more beautiful it becomes, like glass.

When we are carrying impurities, for example sin and bad habits in our hearts, which we keep secret, our hearts and lives have become like impure gold, in an alloy with Satan and his practices.

Today we need to ask ourselves: Are our hearts hard and unusable in the hands of the Lord or soft as pure refined gold?

In Ezekiel 36:26,27, the Lord says that our hearts become like stone when it is full of sin, but He wants to give us a new heart. This heart of stone has often been hardened by legalistic deceitful practices. The purified heart that God wants to give us, will be full of His Spirit and He will write His will and Word on our hearts so that we can live by it, **but we must make the choice whether or not we are willing to give our hearts for the purification process.**

In Ezekiel 18:30-32, the Lord speaks to us urgently, as with Israel of that time, to purify our hearts. The Lord wants to help us, but our sins often stand like a wall between us and Him. He is waiting for us to come to Him so that our hearts may be purified as defined in Isaiah 59:1,2 and 1 John 1:7 and 9.

When the gold is held over the fire, it becomes liquid. A certain substance, called Flux, is added to bring the impurities to the surface.

The goldsmith not only watches the gold but keeps a close eye on it and ensures that the temperature of the fire is exactly right. As soon as the impurities come to the surface, He carefully scoops them off.

It works the same with us.
When we allow the Holy Spirit to work in our hearts, He will convict us of things in our lives that are not for God's glory, of habits and sins of which we are sometimes not even aware of ourselves, but what God can see. The fire with which our hearts are refined is often the trials and tests we go through, as defined in James 1:2-4 & 2 Corinthians 7:1. Under stress and difficult circumstances, our weaknesses are more easily exposed, and we have the opportunity to do something with them. Jesus is intensely interested in us, so He will not allow us to be tested beyond our strength, as promised in 1 Corinthians 10:13.

When the Holy Spirit makes us aware of these unwanted habits and sin that God does not venerate, we have a choice to allow Jesus to wash away the impurity through His blood from our

lives or to continue living in disobedience.... Jesus will only purify our lives when we ask Him to
do so.
Then He removes the impurities from our hearts. 1 John 1:7,9 reminds us of the cleansing
process through Jesus' blood. This is the path of sanctification that Jesus Christ calls us to, as we
see in 1 Thessalonians 4:3,7,8. It is this process of purification that prepares us for eternity.

How does the goldsmith know when the gold is completely purified?
When He can see his own image in the gold! The purification process of our hearts will continue
until Jesus can see His own image fully in our lives.
John 3:30 says, **"He must become more important while I become less important."** This
statement should also be the desire of our hearts.

In 2 Timothy 2:20-21 we are admonished to allow God to purify our hearts and lives so that we
can be an object for His glory. **When our hearts are purified, Jesus is visible in our lives.**

Paul also advises us to put on the Lord Jesus Christ as a robe covering us, as seen in
Romans 13:14. Wearing the robe of Jesus Christ means that **our whole life** must reflect Jesus to
this lost world. All of this begins with the choice of allowing Jesus to purify our lives in this way,
until He can see His Image in us!

Let us make work of ourselves so that our hearts may be like **pure gold in God's hands,** soft,
without rust, shining enough to reflect Jesus in all His glory, so that we may become a vessel
glory unto Him, until the day Jesus comes to fetch us.

*Lord Jesus, today I choose to be purified by Your
caring hands.
I know You will be amid every trial fire,
with me and not let it destroy me.
Loving Abba Father, I know that there is still much
impurity in my life
and that is why I pray
That You may purify me
until You can see Yourself in me.
All to Your glory and honor.
In Jesus' Mighty Name
Amen.*

WHAT DOES THE WHITE CLOTHES, WHICH WE ARE ADVISED TO PURCHASE FROM JESUS, REPRESENT?

Revelation 3:18
Jesus said: "Take My advice and buy gold from Me, refined by fire so you can become rich! <u>Buy from Me white clothing so you can be clothed, and your shameful nakedness will not be exposed,</u> and buy eye salve to put on your eyes so you can see!"

Not all of us love to wear white clothes. It is so impractical in many ways because it can easily get dirty. Yet Jesus specifies that we should not buy any other clothes from Him — they must be **white** robes! What does Jesus really mean here?

In Luke 15:11-23, Jesus tells of a son who claimed his inheritance from his father. This son wasted everything his father gave him through a reckless, loose life. Finally, he loses everything and literally sits among a bunch of dirty, smelly pigs with nothing to eat, dirty and worn clothes on his body, in an absolute precarious state.

That's exactly what happens to us when we turn our backs on the Lord. We enjoy the empty pleasures of sin and in the process, we destroy ourselves. Finally, we sit in the mess of the consequences of sin — broken in spirit, soul, and body, rejected by society. Satan is satisfied that you are now a product of his devastating influence.

This boy decides to go back to his father and confess that he was wrong. He realizes his condition and his unworthiness to be part of the family. His dad does the most wonderful thing!

- His father was waiting for his return. He had already seen him come from afar and ran to welcome him, regardless of his reprehensible, filthy condition — God does the same with us. He is waiting for us to draw close to Him. Read of this in James 4:8 and John 6:44.
- He commands that the boy be clothed in the best robe he has (I believe he was given the opportunity to wash himself clean) – Jesus does the same with us when we approach him. He blots out our transgressions, as Isaiah 43:25 says, and cleanses us with His blood, as seen in 1 John 1:7–9.
- He also ordered that a ring be placed on his finger through which his identity was recovered as confirmation of his family connection. God does the same with us. We become part of His family and by His Spirit we are confirmed, because it is the Holy Spirit who is our mark and seal of our identity in Jesus Christ as described in Ephesians 1:13.
- This Father commands that a feast be prepared that once again affirms his unconditional acceptance & love. In Revelation 3:20, Jesus says that if we heed His knock on our hearts, He will come in and enjoy a meal with us.

When we come back to the Lord and confess our sins, we are washed in the blood of Jesus Christ, clothed in a royal white robe of righteousness. We receive a new identity — Divine identity and a heavenly feast is arranged! When we sit with the Word in our quiet time, the Holy Spirit is ready to share with us a spiritual feast of insight from the Word, the Bible. Jesus, like the father in the story, was also waiting for you to come to His heavenly home.

In Zechariah 3:3-5, Joshua has a vision of the heavenly events and realizes that he has filthy clothes on. He realizes he is unworthy to be in the Lord's presence. God commanded that he is clothed in clean clothes. The Angel (capital "A") of the Lord, which is Jesus Himself, put on clean festive garments for him. Jesus also tells him that his sin debt has been taken away.

What, then, does this white robe represent?
Revelation 19:7-8 gives a clear answer!
"**Let us rejoice and exalt and give Him glory, because the wedding celebration of the Lamb has come, and His bride has made herself ready. She was permitted to be dressed in bright, clean, fine linen" (for the fine linen is the righteous deeds of the saints).**

NB: Who is "the bride" in the verse
The bride represents those who are saved and have a living relationship with Jesus, who kept themselves from sin after being born again.
It points to the children of the Lord who constitutes the church of God. (The Ecclesia Church-those who are truly saved)

"Clean" here refers to being clean of and washed from sin.
"Shiny, fine linen" is symbolic of righteous deeds.

We also see that the people allowed into heaven are all dressed in **WHITE ROBES.**
Revelation 7:9 says: "... **a great multitude, which no man was able to number, out of all nations and tribes and peoples and tongues; they stood before the throne and before the Lamb, clothed in white robes,** and with palm **branches in their hands....**"

Without these white robes, we are spiritually naked before the Lord!
Revelation 16:15 says: "**Behold, I am coming as a thief in the night. Blessed is he that watches, and keeps his garments, lest he walk naked, and they see his shame.**" Jesus Himself says in Revelation 3:18 that we need white robes to cover our (spiritual) nakedness. When we are spiritually naked, our sinful condition is visible before the Lord.

How do I get my life/my clothes clean?
Just one way works and that is, to go to Jesus! He has the answer!
Revelation 7:14b says: "...they have washed their robes and made them white in the blood of the Lamb!" In other words, I/we need to ask Jesus to wash my/our life and heart clean with His blood so that I/we can stand before God, our Father in righteousness! As seen in 1 John 1:7,9 & Isaiah 1:18.
(Interestingly, blood stains our clothes RED and that blood patch, is difficult to wash out of our clothes, BUT when I am washed in the blood of Jesus, I'm white and clean in the spirit!)

What are the righteous acts to which the spiritual white robes are connected??
In Isaiah 61:10 we read that the Lord has put on a garment of righteousness for us. We can only get the robe from Jesus. (Remember, too, what happened to the prodigal son and Joshua in Zechariah.)

We cannot do righteous deeds out of our own strength. God knows this, and He equips us with His Spirit. When I give my heart to Jesus, His Spirit comes to dwell in me. The Holy Spirit is the power in me that helps me do God's will. We see in John 14:26 how the Holy Spirit will teach us and in 2 Corinthians 6:16-18 it is clearly told that we become the temple of God in which He comes to dwell by His Spirit. He also shows that we become His children and He becomes our Father.

As already mentioned, in Romans 13:14 we are advised to clothe ourselves with Jesus Christ. How do I do this? This means that I must develop the character of Jesus in my life. With the Holy Spirit in me, who has the character of Jesus Christ, it takes a choice on my part to allow the Holy Spirit to manifest Jesus' character qualities through me.

Thus, **righteous acts are, to do the things that are in harmony with Jesus ' character and divine will.** These actions are described in various places in Scripture: -

- **Faith** – read Ephesians 2:8; Romans 12:3b; Romans 1:17; Hebrews 11:6
- **True Worship and a living, growing love relationship with Jesus** as defined in John 4:23,24; Matthew 7:19-23
- **Love in practice -** read Colossians 3:12,14; Romans 12:9-21; Romans 5:5, John 13:34,35; 1 John 3:18
- **Living in Forgiveness** – read Colossians 3:13; Matthew 6:14,15
- **Bear the Fruit of the Holy Spirit -** read Galatians 5:22; James 3:17
- **Do good to others** 1 John 3:14; James 2:15,16; Galatians 6:9
- **Tell others about Jesus** Revelation 12:11; Matthew 12:35-37

BUT.........

Are we not only justified by our faith alone as defined in Ephesians 2:8-10 & Romans 1:17?
What about our good works? Do we not deserve eternal life by good works?
Ephesians 2:8,9 says that Faith + Grace + Jesus = Salvation & Eternal Life.
 Yes, it surely is. This faith is at work regarding your salvation in Christ Jesus but must be followed up by "sanctifying faith" which is the result of your salvation in Christ Jesus.

How do I know what you believe??!!
James 2:14-26 explains that faith and works are in fact called righteous deeds....
V. 19 clearly states that demons believe and tremble but do nothing to show their faith!!
Faith must be followed up by works so that everyone can see what you believe!
V. 17 clearly states that faith without works is dead.

Faith and works (righteous deeds & "faith works") take hands, and one cannot function without the other. Therefore, one can use the "spiritual formula" to remember it...

FAITH + RIGHTEOUS DEEDS/FAITHWORKS =
YOUR TESTIMONY TO WHAT AND IN WHOM YOU BELIEVE

Therefore, Jesus could have said that He knew and saw the works of the 7 churches of Revelation, and he could judge, address, and reprove them accordingly.

Do you and I need a white robe?
Yes, of course!
We need to buy the spiritual white robe from Jesus!

HAVE YOU EVER PURCHASED EYE OINTMENT FROM JESUS?

Revelation 3:18
Jesus said: "Take My advice and buy gold from Me, refined by fire so you can become rich! Buy from Me white clothing so you can be clothed, and your shameful nakedness will not be exposed, and buy eye salve to put on your eyes so you can see!"

Laodicea was known for the excellent eye ointment they made for various eye diseases. This eye ointment, they believed, prevented blindness. The Laodicea congregation's blindness was not physical but spiritual in nature. They could not see what their mental and spiritual state looked like. They were blind to their own mental and spiritual flaws and mistakes.

Jesus explains in Matthew 6:22-24 that the lamp of the body is the eye. If we were to look or see wrong things, our bodies would have no light. Our body will then be full of darkness, but if our vision is set correctly, our body will be illuminated.

What did Jesus really mean by this "eye ointment invitation"?
How can my vision be incorrect?
The answer is twofold.
First, we need to ask ourselves – What do you watch on TV or social media? Which books do you read? What are you looking at on the computer?

Second, what knowledge, especially spiritual knowledge accompanied by deep spiritual insight, keeps our minds occupied?

What you see goes inside your body, through your mind processing it to build into your DNA branches and nervous system, which in turn are "engraved" inside your brain. It is stored in your subconscious and in your heart. It will affect your everyday walk and conduct in your life. If you fill yourself and especially your mind with the wrong things like pornography, immorality, murder, and death movies on TV and social media, you can expect that after a long time it's going to affect you and your actions in such a way that you live accordingly. It will become easier to do the wrong things and allow it into our lives. Our minds become so full of the worldly way of living that there is no longer any place left for the Holy Spirit to speak into our lives. It fills our lives with sinful thoughts and practices and as a result our body is spiritually dark.

In Matthew 6, Jesus, in verses 19-21 also speaks of the kinds of treasures that can be stored up. With our eyes, we often desire the physical temporary treasures of this world and focus on gathering it so that we can enjoy life, but its outcome has no value in the Kingdom of God. The treasures we store up in heavenly places are the very ones that we gather through our righteous acts of love.

In Matthew 13:13-15, Jesus also says that the people do not understand what He is saying because they do not allow the Holy Spirit to make it understandable to them. They choose to shut their ears, eyes, and heart for the truth of the gospel of Jesus Christ and the principles of God's Kingdom. Therefore, they will remain spiritually blind, spiritually sick, and poor. They choose not to experience Jesus' healing hand in their spiritual lives.

We all know that if we look directly into the sun without good glasses, we can go blind. Looking and living in the Light of God improves our vision. Moses was constantly in God's presence, and the people could see a brightness of God's Light and glory on his face, so they asked him to cover his face. Yet we read that Moses never went blind. At 120 years old, his eyes were still as strong as when he was a young man. Read of this in Deuteronomy 34:7.

We see in Hebrews 11:8-12 that Abraham's faith was so strong that he had a spiritual vision. A vision with which he expected the city with firm foundations, of which God is the Builder and Maker.

How can spiritual blindness be restored?
Your vision is determined by your deep insight into God's Word that will eventually also restore your spiritual blindness.

We see that Jesus regularly identified the Pharisees as blind leaders. Read of it in Matthew 15:14 and Matthew 23:16,24. What made these spiritual leaders so blind? **They were trapped in the legalistic lifestyle of the Old Testament and not at all receptive to the new doctrine and Gospel of Jesus Christ and the Kingdom of God.** They also blinded the people who followed them by making them adherents to the same traditions and laws.

2 Corinthians 3:12-18 explains and further confirms this fact: "Therefore, since we have such a hope, we behave with great boldness, and not like Moses who used to put a veil over his face to keep the Israelites from staring at the result of the glory that was made ineffective, but their minds were closed *(Their spiritual vision and insight were obscured and blinded.)* **For to this very day, the same veil remains when they hear the old covenant** *(Old Testament and the law)* **read**. It has not been removed because **only in Christ is it taken away,** but until this very day whenever Moses is read *(the Old Testament and the law)*, a veil lies over their minds *(their minds and heart are blinded for the doctrine of Jesus Christ, no new spiritual insight/vision can develop in Jesus Christ because of the spiritual blindness)*, **but when one turns to the Lord, the veil is removed.** *(New spiritual insight/vision is given by the Holy Spirit.)* **Now the Lord is the Spirit, and where the Spirit of the Lord is present, there is freedom.** And we all, with unveiled faces reflecting the glory of the Lord, are being transformed into the same image from one degree of glory to another, which is from the Lord, who is the Spirit. *(Jesus Christ destroys the spiritual blindness and gives us this new vision!)*

Jesus invites us to buy "eye ointment" from Him.
Remember, eye salvage consists of different ingredients that work healingly on the eyes. The base of eye ointment is an oil that will not damage the eye. Likewise, the "eye ointment" Jesus offers us is also made up of different ingredients.

THE EYE OINTMENT THAT JESUS OFFERS US...
It contains different spiritual ingredients: -
- An Oil base which represents the presence of the Holy Spirit
The Holy Spirit provides us with deep spiritual insight, wisdom, knowledge and understanding as revealed from God. He reveals God's secrets to us. Read about this in Isaiah 11:2 & Ephesians 1:18
- Psalm 146:8 tells us that it is only our Lord who can heal our spiritual blindness
Healing comes by spending quality time with Him and His Word, the Bible.
Personal Quality time with Jesus results in deep spiritual vision and insight. Combined with prayer and praise and worship in your personal place for meeting with the Lord will provide the spiritual healing for blindness. The more time you spend with Jesus, the more you will be able to hear His voice and understand His message.
Faith provides spiritual vision as well as physical vision - see Matthew 9:28,29 & Hebrews 11:1,13,20,27. According to Numbers 14:6-11, we see that Joshua & Caleb surely had vision of faith. Our physical vision of circumstances must be dominated by our vision of faith and spiritual vision of Jesus and on His ability. Faith vision also comes with hearing the Word of God which is confessed as Paul teaches us in Romans 10:17.

A choice for spiritual vision

The day when we give our hearts to the Lord and His Spirit comes to dwell in us, is the day when God comes to dwell in us in all His fullness. Yet God is waiting for us to choose to obey the voice of His Spirit. He wants to speak to us through His Spirit, teach us, and guide us.

We see repeatedly how the Holy Spirit works through people in various ways, after they have been anointed with oil: -

> ➢ Leviticus 14:14-18 - The priest anoints the person's right earl (hearing), on his right thumb (deeds), right great toe (walking in God's principles), and on his forehead (minding godly thoughts and receiving them from the Lord), after the cleansing process is completed. In this way, the sensitivity to the guidance of the Holy Spirit is confirmed in the person's life.
> ➢ 1 Samuel 10:1,6,11 - Samuel anoints Saul as king of Israel. Verse 6 says that Saul's life initially changed. He acted differently than in the past. He even prophesied, but after a time he chose not to listen to the voice of God's Spirit anymore and the Holy Spirit abandoned him.
> ➢ 2 Kings 6:15-17 - Elisha prays for his servant so that he can receive spiritual vision. It is God's Spirit who has worked this vision.
> ➢ Acts 2:3,4 and Acts 4:31 - The disciples are empowered by the Holy Spirit to tell others about Jesus. The Holy Spirit also gives them a fearless spirit.
> ➢ Acts 8:15-17 - After people had given their hearts to the Lord, the apostles laid their hands on them and prayed for them so that the Holy Spirit could actively begin to work in them.
> ➢ James 5:14-15 - Shows that we can anoint sick people and lay hands on them and pray so that they may be healed.
> ➢ 1 John 2:27 - Shows us that we will be taught by the anointing of the Holy Spirit by the word of God and will understand things, because the Holy Spirit explains it to us.

It is important to understand that in the Old Testament the Holy Spirit came upon the people for a brief time, but in the New Testament we see that **God's Spirit comes to dwell in us and work in us**, sanctification.

Do we need the Holy Spirit?

Yes, indeed! Jesus tells us to buy ointment from Him for our eyes. The Holy Spirit gives us the ability to understand the deeper things of God's Word, to see and realize the truth of ourselves and our circumstances, to have faith vision, to do things that are not possible in our own strength and give us the strength to obey God regardless of our circumstances.

Answer this question in the secret closet of your heart: Have you invited the Holy Spirit to work freely in your life? He will, if you invite Him or ask Him.

"Therefore, having so great a cloud of witnesses surrounding us, let us also put off every weight and the sin that so easily surrounds us, and let us run with endurance the race that is set before us, our eyes intent on Jesus, the Author and Perfecter of faith, who is for the joy set before Him, the cross endured, despised shame, and sat down at the right hand of the throne of God." Hebrews 12:1-2

Let us strive to gain new spiritual vision in Jesus Christ through the workings of His Spirit.

Father God, thank you for sending Jesus
to teach us about You.

Jesus, thank you for coming and giving us Your Spirit.
so that You can be so close to us.
Holy Spirit thank you for coming to teach us more
about Jesus and Abba Father.
I pray that you will work anew in my life and
open my eyes to see and understand the divine things.
Please drench me from head to toe
so that I will be an object to Abba Father's glory.
I know that you will work within me and
provide me with a steadfast spirit in Jesus, and
that you will always set my eyes on Jesus Christ,
the Beginning and End of my faith.
Please lead me into the truth and
be the fire that burns in my heart and motivates me.
towards an intimate love relationship with Jesus
until the day He comes to get us.
In The Name of Jesus,
Amen.

WITH WHAT CURRENCY WILL WE BE ABLE TO PURCHASE THESE GOODS FROM JESUS?

Haggai 2:8
"The silver and gold will be mine,' says the LORD who rules overall."

Psalm49:7-9
"Certainly, a man cannot rescue his brother;
he cannot pay God an adequate ransom price
(the ransom price for a human life is too high,
and people go to their final destiny),
so that he might continue to live forever
and not experience death."

What is valuable enough in the Lord's eyes to use as a "currency" for purchasing from Him?
The silver, gold, and money belong to the Lord anyway. He is, after all, the Creator of the Universe! If I, have it, I can't offer it.

What did Jesus use to buy us?
1 Timothy 2:5,6
"For there is one God and one Mediator between God and men, the man <u>Christ Jesus, who gave Himself as a ransom for all...</u>"

From whom did Jesus have to buy us?
A ransom is paid when a slave is bought free from his master.
In John 8:34, Jesus explains that we are servants/slaves of sin. We are slaves to Satan and caught up in the law of the Old Testament which judge us. Romans 3:23 says that we have all sinned.

A slave could not redeem himself and had to do all that his master commanded him. He was the property of his owner for life. The only way to escape is if someone else pays a ransom for him with the intention of releasing him.

In John 8:36, Jesus says He wants to set us free so that we can be truly free. This freedom is worked, among other things, by the Truth He has come to offer us.

Jesus bought us by paying for you and me with His life on the cross. He died and rose from the dead, redeeming you and me free from sin and free from the grip of Satan! Jesus not only bought us to be free but also offers us access to eternal life.

<u>What is precious enough for the Lord so that we will be able to purchase something from Him?</u>
1 Peter 2:21says, **"For to this end you have been called... that Christ left you an example, that you might follow in His** steps." Just as Jesus did, so should we.

Therefore, we can buy from Jesus in the following way: -
We buy from Jesus by offering our Whole Life (spirit, soul, and body) as a "currency"! We give **<u>ourselves as Jesus gave Himself as a ransom for us</u>**. Jesus gave his all. We can't just give half of ourselves and think that's enough. James 4:4 warns us that we cannot be a friend of the

world and a friend of God at the same time, because there is enmity between the world and God. It's all or nothing!

In Mark 12:29-31, Jesus says to the people:
"Hear Israel, **the Lord our God, is one Lord; And thou shalt love the Lord thy God with all thy heart, and with all thy soul, and with all thy mind, and with all thy strength.** This is the first commandment.
And the second is like this: **You shall love your neighbor as yourself. There is no other commandment greater than this.**"
This verse implies **a total surrender to the Lord**, in spirit, soul, and body.

When you surrender yourself to Jesus in this way, He does exactly what we are invited to buy from Him in Revelation 3:18: -
- ❖ He purifies our heart until it is like precious pure gold in His hands.
- ❖ He gives you the ability to do righteous deeds, in other words you will wear the white robe.
- ❖ He gives you His Spirit as anointing for your eyes so that you can gain spiritual insight, wisdom, knowledge and understanding. (Enlightened eyes of the mind – read Ephesians 1:18)

When we surrender to Jesus, we enjoy the privileges of childhood in a godly family, for Jesus bought us from the bondage of sin and the influence of the law so that we could be ushered into the freedom of a divine identity. This fact is confirmed in our hearts by His Spirit, when we read **Romans 8:15-17** that says: "**For all who are led by the Spirit of God are the sons of God. For you did not receive the spirit of slavery leading again to fear, but you received the Spirit of adoption, by whom we cry, "Abba, Father**.
The **Spirit Himself bears witness to our spirit that we are God's children and if children, then heirs (namely, heirs of God and also fellow heirs with Christ) – if indeed we suffer with Him so we may also be glorified with Him.**"

I want to challenge you today to serve God
with everything in you and hold nothing back and
see if you won't then enjoy the abundant blessings
from His hand. I know you will!

In John 1:12-13 it is written: "But to all who have received Him – those who believe in His Name – He has given the right to become God's children – children not born by human parents or by human desire or a husband's decision, but by God."

"For you were bought at a price. Therefore, glorify God with your body".
1 Corinthians 6:20

Take the first step toward a true life in Jesus Christ and
be born again by His Spirit.
Please read John 3:5-6,16,18 to hear about this birth.

THE DOOR

Revelation 3:20
"Listen! I am standing at the door and knocking!
If anyone hears My voice and opens the door
I will come into him and share a meal with him, and he with Me"

When faced with an open or closed door, we have several choices to make. If the door is closed, we can knock and may be invited in, or turn around and walk away. If the door is open, we must choose to walk in through the door or turn away and not enter.

Sometimes we look for a door in a strange environment that will bring us to our planned destination. It's the door that leads to a planned appointment where someone is waiting to meet with us.

The opposite can also happen, namely, that someone comes knocking on our house, office, or room door and we have the choice to open and invite in, or to ignore the knock as if we haven't heard it.

Which side of the door we stand, can also determine where we stand in life and what we experience. For the disobedient child, the door to the principal's office is one that leads to pain, guidance and anxiety; For the criminal, the prison is through one that leads to captivity; For the young man or woman at university, the doors to success and prosperity for the future lead to the realization of their dreams; For the bird trapped in the bird cage, the open door is the way to freedom.

However, there are other doors as well. Doors that are visible only in the spiritual dimension. These doors are often far more important than any door in this world.

For Adam and Eve, after the fall into sin, **the door leading to** the garden of Eden, was shut, never to be opened again. The closing of this door by God, was an act of grace and mercy, although it was not understood fully by humanity at that time It was a sad day that changed the lives of Adam and Eve, as well as the lives of humanity after them, forever. Read about this incident in Genesis 3:17,23,24.

Disobedience and sin prevailed among mankind, and each time sin knocked on their hearts' door, they opened without resistance and invited sin in and did as their hearts desired. Read about it in Genesis 4:7b.

A unique day dawns in which God engages with Noah and reveals to him his plan to destroy the earth with water, due to the sins of mankind. He commanded him to build an ark that would become the means by which he would save and protect Noah, his family and the animals. Noah and his family were the only ones of that time who found grace in God's eyes because they did not give in to the sin that came knocking on their hearts' door. In Genesis 6:8 and 9, we see that Noah was counted as a righteous, upright man among his contemporaries. We are told here that Noah walked with God. This testimony opened a divine door for Noah and his family, while the same door closed for the other people who refused to live in line with God's will.

During this event, we discover a door that is directly in relation to God's grace. After Noah, his family, and the animals entered the ark, God Himself shuts the door behind them. Read about it in Genesis 7:16. It took Noah 120 years to finish building the ark, and at that time the people heard the warnings of this "judgement" day which God told him about, every day. It was a period of grace in which the people could turn their hearts back to God, but they mocked Noah and rejected the call of repentance. God shut the **door to grace,** and the people finally lost their chance to salvation. What a scary day!

Many years later, we see in Jonah 1:2 & Jonah 3:3-10 & Jonah 4:2b that a similar situation is taking place in the city of Nineveh. The inhabitants of this city, along with its king, are warned by Jonah that God will destroy the city because of their wickedness. These people repent of their sinful practices and God shows them mercy by withdrawing His judgment of destruction. For these people, **the door of grace remained open**.

God desires to wipe out the separation of sin between Himself and man and begins to pave the way to the greatest Door of all doors. A door that He, Himself sets up for us, to open the way to eternal life with Him. This plan already came into action since Genesis.

In Exodus 25 we read how the Lord instructed Moses to erect the Tabernacle. We see how the Lord miraculously prepares mankind for the coming of His Son, Jesus, in a wonderful way, hundreds of years before the coming of His Son.

Jesus is the true Door to a restored relationship with God. The unique characteristics of each **entrance or door of the Tabernacle,** from the Courtyard to the Sanctuary and Most Holy, as well as the practices within the Tabernacle, were finger-pointing to **Jesus Christ,** Who at last, was not only the perfect sacrifice for our sins, but also that **Door,** through which we would have to walk to get in harmony with God, to obtain our salvation and to inherit eternal life. When we go to God through Jesus, we can experience His presence in our lives.

Jesus plainly states in John 10:9: **"I am the door; If anyone enters by Me, he will be saved and will go in and go out and find pasture."**

Our sinful condition requires a sinless perfect sacrifice, the blood of a sinless "Being," Jesus Christ, to open the door of grace to God's presence. Read Hebrews 9:14,24,26; Hebrews 7:25 & Hebrews 4:14-16. **Jesus becomes not only the embodiment of God's grace, but also the Manifestation of His grace and love for a humanity that it cannot merit in any other way. However, the responsibility rests on every human being to make the final choice to walk through the Door of God's grace, through Jesus Christ, who is the Door to a restored relationship with God, our Eternal Father and Creator, or not.** The potential on the other side of this Grace Door is breathtakingly great!

As we walk through this Door of Grace, we not only meet our Creator and Eternal Father, but discover other new spiritual doors that God has set up for us to grow our relationship with Him. Each door takes us to a deeper, yet higher level of intensity in our relationship with God. Still, it remains our choice to diligently search for these doors, open them, and walk through or not. Of course, this will determine the level of our relationship with God.

Another important door, the **Door of Faith** that leads to salvation, deliverance and healing as well as various other miracles from God's loving hand. Faith comes by hearing the Word of God, as defined in Romans 10:17. Without faith, it is impossible to please God and enjoy His favor in our lives. Read about it in Hebrews 11:6.

The **Door of Faith** opens the **Door of our Lips** so that we will confess our conviction in Jesus, our Savior with surrender and sincerity. Read Psalm 14:3 & Romans 10:9-11,13.

The **Door of our Lips** leads us to the **Doors of Praise** and **Doors of Spiritual Victories as well as the Door of Freedom in Christ.** When we look at Paul and Silas in Acts 16:25,26-36, we see 2 missionaries who have been savagely mistreated by the people because they dare to open the door of their lips and preach salvation in Christ Jesus.

It is midnight, and Paul and Silas don't let pain, guidance, and discouragement shut their mouths and shut the prison doors. They begin to bring praise to Jesus Christ. This not only becomes a testimony to fellow prisoners but moves God's powerful hand. Their midnight sacrifice of praise becomes the powerful key that unlocks the prison doors to freedom and spiritual victory. **"And about midnight Paul and Silas prayed and sang praises to God; And the prison listened. And suddenly a great earthquake came, so that the foundations of the prison were shaken. And immediately all the doors were opened, and the bonds of all were loosed."** Acts 16:25,26.

The jailer and his family come to repentance, the prisoners are also introduced to **Jesus, our Eternal Door,** and all of them have the opportunity to rectify their relationship with God and to share in eternal life.

When we live according to the will of God, we can expect God to open and shut spiritual doors for us. Paul testifies in 1 Corinthians 16:9: **"For a mighty door has opened to me, and there are many adversaries."** Although we, like Paul, can engage in spiritual warfare, we are always assured of God's supporting right hand. He promises that "the angel of the Lord draws a camp around those who fear him, and he delivers them." Psalm 34:8. **When Jesus opens or closes doors, it is a powerful and sure matter. No human being or evil can change that**. Revelation 3:7,8. Therefore, we need not fear when we face a spiritual door. We don't just walk through it. God is always with you.

In Matthew 25:10-13, Jesus tells the parable of the 10 virgins invited to the wedding feast. Five of the virgins bring along extra oil to ensure that they have enough to get to the moment the Bridegroom of all time arrives. The other five virgins did not take extra oil with them and ended up in crisis due to a shortage of oil. They urgently need to go and buy more oil and miss the moment the Bridegroom finally arrives. We are like these 10 virgins. Some of us work diligently on our relationship with God so that the Holy Spirit can continually work powerfully in and through us. Others are lax again, only occasionally making time to maintain their relationship with God. How tragic it is that this very group, who with the unexpected coming of the Bridegroom, namely Jesus, miss out on the breathtaking occasion. Worst of all, we are so busy with the temporary obligations that we don't even notice His coming! When we do realize that He has come, we face a CLOSED DOOR! The **door is already locked** and it's too late!! We missed our chances! What a shocking experience that will be! The latter 5 virgins faced this shocking reality and had to hear these words: **"Truly I say to you, I do not know you."** **Matthew 25:11,12.**

In Revelation 3:20, we read that Jesus is knocking on **your heart's door**. As He knocks on, He calls you by name to open. What are you going to do? Are you going to shut the **door of your heart** and ignore the cry of Jesus? Perhaps you say to yourself: "Oh, I don't have time for this right now! It's for another day... Now is not the right time. I still have so many other things to do and my whole life lies ahead of me to enjoy."

Friend, I urge you to reflect on this very important decision you need to make. Why do you want to miss out on the best and most fulfilling life ever? The Bridegroom, Jesus is on His way, and you may just miss His coming and find yourself in front of a locked Grace Door!

Is it worth missing the chance to live in the eternal presence of God, for the temporary pleasures of this world?

Where God is, true peace, and perfect love, prevails and one day no more sorrow, pain, or sickness, and death will exist. Only LIFE, true Life – Eternal Life!!

Choose today not to turn away from the Door of Grace. Open your heart's door and invite Jesus inside. Jesus promises that together you will enjoy a spiritual feast. A feast with eternal value!

Jesus is knocking at your heart's door today.
Do you hear him calling?
Don't wait, answer Him and open your door.
You won't regret it!

"TODAY, IF YOU HEAR MY VOICE...
HARDEN NOT YOUR HEARTS"

Hebrews 3:7-8
"Therefore, as the Holy Spirit says,
"Oh, that today you would listen as He speaks!
Do not harden your hearts as in the rebellion,
In the day of testing in the wilderness."

We read the full story, which gave rise to the above statement, in Exodus 17:1-7.
The Israelites rebelled against God and against Moses, for they were weary and thirsty in the wilderness, and according to them, all of this is Moses and the Lord's fault! They are so rebellious and arrogant that they question the presence of God in their midst! That's a big mistake! Yet the Lord blessed them and had Moses and the elders of Israel separated so that He could speak to them and confirm His presence and miracle-working power to them.
He does not speak to the rebellious people, but to those whose hearts would be receptive.
He waits for them at mount Horeb and supplies water from the rocks.

The presence of sin, which in principle is rebellion against God, leads to a hardened heart and makes us, among other things, spiritually deaf to the voice of the Lord.

For children of the Lord, communication between God and us should be of utmost importance, since it is an integral part of a living, growing relationship with Him.
BUT
People search for other sources of communication to tell them about the Lord. It leads them on a wandering path that just once again progressively separates them from the Lord while they cling to deceitful dogma.

COMMUNICATION IN THE OLD AND THE NEW TESTAMENT
In the **OLD TESTAMENT**, we see that God made contact with people in various ways.

As early as the garden of Eden, we see that He visited Adam and Eve in the evening breeze. We read about this in **Genesis 3:8.**

Later, we see that His communication was through dreams, visions, angels, judges, prophets, a pillar of cloud, fire, and deportation.
Examples of this are found in: -
Daniel 10:12-14; Judges 6:12-27
> The Lord sends an angel to deliver His message.
1 King 19:11-13
> The Lord's presence is powerful in nature, but when He speaks to us, it is usually gentle and calm — "in the sound of a gentle "cool silence" the voice of the Lord is audible.
Numbers 22:26-35
> God speaks through a donkey and later opens Balaam's eyes so that he can see the Angel speaking to him.
Job 33:14-16
> God speaks through dreams and visions.
Numbers 12:6,8
> God speaks through dreams, visions, and word.
Isaiah 6:1-11
> Visions and visitations in the Spirit.

Much of **the <u>Old Testament generation experienced a strong visual manifestation of the Deity,</u> in which God made His <u>message known.</u>**

In the **NEW TESTAMENT,** we see less of these incidents and a more **inner and personal form** of communication, from, and with the Holy Spirit. Especially after the outpouring of the Holy Spirit in Acts 2, we see a strong working, communication, and presence of the Holy Spirit in people's lives. It is, of course, the fulfillment of Jesus' prediction of the outpouring of His Spirit before He returns to heaven.

In Joel 2:28-32, we are warned that the Holy Spirit will be poured out in great measure, giving rise to visions, dreams, prophecies in the end-time. It begins in Acts 2. Peter refers to this in his sermon in Acts 2:17-21.

In 1 Corinthians 6:19 and 2 Corinthians 6:16-18, we see the reason for the changed way of communication. **The indwelling of God's Spirit within man as His temple, results in a personal form of communication as the preferred method by God's Spirit.**

DIVINE COMMUNICATION IN THE PRESENT ERA
Today, however, we see a very confused picture of so-called communication between God and men while people do not bother to truly build a true, living relationship with God, in spirit and truth, first. Their search for a Supreme Being takes them on stray tracks far away from the Lord.

This spiritual confusion is reinforced by **ignorance** concerning God's Word that worsens because of **misinformation, propaganda, and deception.** This makes it difficult then to distinguish between the true truth that leads to eternal life and a relationship with Jesus, and the lies of the world and the evil one.

<u>God's truth is the only stable factor by which we will be able to discern the lies of the world and the wicked</u>.

People choose to adhere to religions that suit their lifestyle. This makes them lend their ears to a multitude of teachers who will fulfill and approve of their own lusts. In this way, they turn their ears away from the truth of God's Word and cling to fables that will soothe their hearing. Please read 2 Timothy 4:3-4 where Paul warns against this.

In 1 Corinthians 12 and 1 Corinthians 14, we see the manifestation of the Holy Spirit within the congregation where it was practiced for the building up and establishment of the congregation. Paul explains here how this should function in practice, as order was needed within the congregation. These manifestations were in the form of gifts of grace as described in 1 Corinthians 12 where Paul describes them as follows:
- message of wisdom,
- the message of knowledge,
- faith,
- healing,
- performance of miracles,
- prophecy,
- discernment of spirits,
- different kinds of tongues, and
- interpretation of tongues.

These gifts are not ours to possess but is part of the manifestations of the Holy Spirit within us. The Holy Spirit works from within us outwardly to reflect the mighty presence of God.

Unfortunately, these manifestations are abused in many of the modern churches and hijacked by Satan to further deceive the people with a counterfeit version. Even within these so-called Christian churches, practices are practiced that the Lord has already condemned and abhorred in the Old Testament era.

It has become vital to return to the most important source of communication between God and man... HIS SPOKEN WORD... THE BIBLE!

<u>THE MOST IMPORTANT SOURCE AND FORM OF COMMUNICATION BETWEEN GOD AND MAN</u>
2 Timothy 3:16-17 tells us plainly: "Every Scripture is inspired by God and useful for teaching, for reproof, for correction, and for training in righteousness, that the person dedicated to God may be capable and equipped for every good work."

This is where we will truly be able to hear the voice of the Lord if our heart, spirit, and soul are open and receptive to His voice and message.

It is through hearing His word that faith is **generated in our hearts.** Read Romans 10:17.

God's spoken word is powerful enough to save our souls, explains James in James 1:21, which says:
"Wherefore lay apart (renounce) all filthiness and superfluity of naughtiness, and **receive with meekness the engrafted word, which is able to save your souls."**
James further writes and exhorts in verses 22-25 that we **should not only be hearers of the word of the Lord but must be doers of the word.** We must measure **ourselves in word and deed by God's Word and make needed changes, under the guidance of the Holy Spirit** so that we will live for God's glory. Moreover, we **can receive deep insight into the perfect law of freedom, and should we live by it, we will be happy and blessed in what we do.**

Jesus says in John 8:34 to the believing Jews and also to us, **"Then Jesus said to those Judeans who had believed him, "<u>If you continue to follow my teaching, you are really my disciples and you will know the truth, and the truth will set you free."</u>** Here lies one of the keys to knowing the true truth and living in it. Jesus confirms the fact that we must not only be hearers of His word, but <u>become believing doers</u>, so that we can throw off the chains and bondage of law and sin and live in the freedom He offers.

God's powerful spoken Word is unchanging and thus the only stable factor in our lives amid an extremely variable world, so it is important to spend time with the Lord and His Word, the Bible.

HOW DO I HEAR THE VOICE OF THE LORD?
In her book, Rebekah Brown explains how it works and how we can condition ourselves to hear the voice of the Lord.

The Holy Spirit will communicate the message of the Lord to our spirit. It is transformed into our minds into understandable words and deposited there.
We have the choice to heed the word or message of the Lord or not.
If we heed to the voice and message of the Holy Spirit, we will discover that He will more often speak to us. If we ignore Him, the opposite will be true -we will hear His voice less.

Method of hearing and knowing the voice of the Holy Spirit: -
We can learn some unknown Bible verses and ask the Holy Spirit to remind us of the verses at a time when we are not at all busy with spiritual things, such as at work or in a store. This is going to mean that the Holy Spirit must interrupt our line of thought at that moment and bring the verses into our minds so that we remember them. When that happens, we will know it's the Holy Spirit who does this and we'll be able to discern His voice more clearly. The more we apply this "exercise" in our lives, the stronger our faith becomes and the clearer we will hear His voice.

HOW DO I KNOW IF IT IS JESUS TALKING THROUGH HIS SPIRIT TO ME?
- The message will always be in line with God's character.
- The message will be confirmed by the Word of the Lord/the Bible.
- It will be in line with God's will.
- You will experience the peace of the Lord and sometimes an urgency to do in obedience what He asks.
- You can ask for confirmation for the message/word you received. Gideon did that. Read the event in Judges 6:12-27,34 & v36-40.

Be warned! Watch out for the next...
1.   **Galatians 1:7** People can distort the Gospel. Examine the Scriptures to know the truth of God.
2.   **2 Corinthians 11:13-14** Beware of people who utter false words while posing as children of the Lord. Satan deceives us by coming as an angel of light.
3.   **2 Timothy 3:5** People who present themselves as holy but deny the Lord.
4.   **Matthew 24:23-27** Jesus warns against erroneous teachings and prophets who present themselves as Christ.
5.   **2 Timothy 2:15** People who walk and live in the Truth and do it themselves will rightly convey the Word of God.

DOES THE LORD ALSO SPEAK TO UNSAVED PEOPLE?
Yes, he speaks to them so that they can repent and become His children.
However, man must choose whether to heed the voice of the Lord or not.
First, God draws the people to Him through someone who brings a sermon or through someone who does a good deed that displays God's love to someone, or the Word is somehow sown in the person's heart.
Read John 6:44,65b. After that, the Holy Spirit begins to work in their hearts to convict them of sin, judgment, and righteousness as defined in John 16:8-11.

WHY WOULD JESUS CHRIST WANT TO TALK TO ME?
- ❖ From the beginning of creation, we see that God visited man to cultivate a living relationship with Him. Genesis 3:8.

- ❖ 2 Corinthians 6:16 the Lord reiterates His desire to connect with us as with a friend and family member. He wants to be with us and in us. He wants to be a Father to us, caring, loving, and much more.

- ❖ We are very precious to God. So precious that He was willing to sacrifice His Son so that the relationship destroyed by sin could be restored between us and Him. We are like His apple of the eye, and He wants to remember us and think of us constantly. Therefore, our names are engraved in the palm of His hand. See Deuteronomy 32:10b; Isaiah 49:16.

- ❖ God wants to reveal His plans to us. See Psalm 25:14; Jeremiah 33:3. Note the prophetic books in the Bible such as Isaiah, Daniel, Ezekiel, and Revelation that reveal the things to come to us.

❖ God speaks to us to motivate us to take pro-active action when He warns us about our sinful practices and how He wants to punish us if we don't repent. A characteristic of God's Word in this aspect is that His warnings are not merely judgmental and damning. God always gives us a promise of reconciliation and blessing if we repent of our wrongdoing. Read Isaiah 1:16-19; Jeremiah 29:13,14

❖ God wants to encourage us, comfort us, and make His love for us, known to us.

❖ God sees in you and me the potential He Himself has deposited in our lives to do for the glory of His Name and wants to encourage us to develop and live it to the fullest, knowing that it will work for our fulfillment and happiness. Read Jeremiah 29:11.

WHAT CAN PREVENT ME FROM HEARING THE VOICE OF THE LORD?
- Sin in my life - Isaiah 59:1–2
- Unbelief - Hebrews 3:10
- Rebellion, rebelliousness, hardening of heart. - Hebrews 3:13 & Exodus 17:1-7
- Bitterness - Hebrews 12:14,15
- Disobedience - 1 Samuel 15:22-23
- Our upset emotions regarding a matter of which we are not hearing the voice of the Lord.
- Spiritual War - Daniel 10:2-6,12-14
- Unforgiveness – Colossians 3:13
- Interference of Satan in our world of thought by creating in our minds wrong and twisted impressions and opinions, which do not harmonize with God's will and character. Therefore, it is necessary to break down these strongholds regularly by taking our minds captive to obedience to Christ and putting on the helmet of salvation. Read about this conduct in 2 Corinthians 10:4,5 & Ephesians 6:17.

Remember, the Holy Spirit has been given by God to the person who has an **obedient heart**. He dwells within our heart and confirms our witness. Read about it in Acts 5:29-32b.

WHY SHOULD I HEAD TO THE VOICE OF THE LORD? PEOPLE ARE TALKING TO ME TOO! ATTITUDE PROBLEM!!
God is great, sovereign, almighty, our Creator, and can do far beyond what we can think or comprehend. There is no one like Him. We should be honored that He is interested in us.

We need to cultivate a receptive attitude. With such an attitude, we will have a tender heart, which is not hardened by the presence of sin and who is willing to be subject to God, like a little child to His parents.

In Hebrews 3:7,8,15, and Psalm 95:7, we see that the presence of rebellion has hardened the hearts of the people of Israel and will do the same to our hearts. Their actions showed this hardening towards the Lord. God speaks to Moses whose heart was receptive to the Lord and it is only God's grace and love that makes Him yet take care of them in the wilderness.

In Jonah 1:1-3,5 we see Jonah at first refusing to obey the voice of the Lord and flee in the hope that he will be able to hide from God. He did not want to do what God told him, and this led to him being disciplined by God to the point of obedience. Even God's chastisement was not an act of lovelessness, but an opportunity to a second chance to obey. In the midst of His chastening, we see God's grace, love, and miracle-working hand in the life of Jonah, but also toward the people of Nineveh. God wanted to show Nineveh mercy.

Moses' gentle heart toward the Lord made his relationship with the Lord one of intense friendship, within which Moses could have the boldness to persuade God to change His decisions. Read about it in Exodus 32:31-33. Exodus 33:7-23 & Exodus 34:5-10.

What is your attitude when God speaks to you?

DO YOU WANT TO HEAR THE VOICE OF THE LORD?

How is your relationship with Jesus? Is it just a one-way communication with Him or is there dialogue?? Are we perhaps too busy with the temporary things of this world rather than making time in which the Lord can speak to us? If so, it is time to reflect on our relationship with Jesus. Personally, we would not be satisfied if our children or friends would only want to know us when they wanted something from us, but now we expect God to be content with such a relationship.

Two-way communication is an integral part of a healthy, happy, fulfilling relationship between two parties. This is especially true in our relationship with the Jesus.

What do I need to do to cultivate a healthy relationship with the Jesus?

- Maintain an active, growing relationship with the Lord.
- Drench yourself with the Word, the Bible.
- Make yourself receptive to when God speaks to you.
- You will also be able to identify God's voice more easily.
- Make sure that your prayer life also contains dialogue i.e., become completely silent so that God can speak to you.
- Measure prophecies, word, dreams, visions against Biblical criteria and guidelines.
- Be obedient to God's commands.
- Do not ignore the voice of the Lord. In the end, it falls into the same category as disobedience.

When God sees your sincere obedience, the incidents in which He speaks to you, become more.

Jesus tells a parable in Matthew 21:28-32 in which a father's two sons respond differently to his request that they go to work in his vineyard. The first son refuses from the outset to do what his father asks, but later repents and goes to work in the vineyard. The second son agrees to work in the vineyard but does not.

We often act like the second son and do not always think about the fact that it grieves the Lord. Revelation 3:14-18 warns us to make sure that our relationship with the Lord is not one of hypocrisy. A heart of refined, pure gold ensures that our heart is gentle and receptive to the Lord. We can then expect to hear the voice of the Lord. God wants to communicate with us and reveal His secrets to us but is looking for people who will focus on Him in obedience. Please read Acts 5:32b; Psalm 25:14; Jeremiah 33:3 deals with this.

We have boldness to share our secrets with a friend, when we feel that we can trust the person that appeal to us. Such a friendship can only develop when the two persons spend a lot of time together and are focused on building their friendship. This also applies in our relationship with the Jesus.

1 Corinthians 6:17 says that the person who clings to the Lord is one spirit with Him, while Psalm 25:14 explains that the Lord reveals His secrets to those who fear Him.

Billy Graham asked the Lord why He called him for the great task the Lord had given him. The Lord's answer was that He called two other people, but they did not heed His cry. God will not shipwreck His plan for this world's salvation because of the reluctance of man. He chooses someone who is willing to heed His cry.

The anointing of the Holy Spirit rests on those who are willing to listen to God and heed His cry and Word. See 1 John 2:20,27. They will be led by His Spirit and the Truth will be revealed to them so that they can glorify God in all things and bring others to Him through the testimony that the Holy Spirit will put in their mouths. John 16:13 and Luke 12:12.

Jesus repeatedly said in His time here on earth: "**He who has ears to hear, let him hear**."
See Matthew 13:9.
Jesus further pointed out in Matthew 13:13-15 that the people's hearts were not receptive to His message to them. It is sad because they missed many other blessings from the Lord.

James exhorts us to be quick to hear and slow to speak. See it in James 1:19.

*Let us heed this exhortation and work diligently
to have a receptive heart for the voice of the Lord.*

QUALITY COMMUNICATION BETWEEN GOD & YOU, AN IMPORTANT PART OF A GODLY RELATIONSHIP

Isaiah 55:3,6,8,9
Pay attention and come to Me!
<u>Listen, so you can live!</u>
Then I will make an unconditional covenantal promise to you,
Just like the reliable covenantal promises I made to David
<u>Seek the LORD while He makes Himself available;</u>
<u>call to Him while He is nearby!</u>
Indeed, My plans are not like your plans,
and My deeds are not like your deeds,
for just as the sky is higher than the earth,
so My deeds are superior to your deeds
and My plans superior to your plans," says the Lord.

<u>**QUALITY COMMUNICATION CONSISTS OF SEVERAL IMPORTANT COMPONENTS THAT ALSO APPLY IN YOUR RELATIONSHIP WITH THE LORD.**</u>

<u>**Communication components include the following: -**</u>
- ❖ Listen carefully to what is being said.
- ❖ Take short notes to remember better.
- ❖ Focus on actively listening and not looking for reason to counter answer.
- ❖ Be open and receptive to the message conveyed.
- ❖ Do not allow distractibility.
- ❖ Be sure to accurately understand what is being said and what the message entails.
- ❖ Communication takes place between at least two parties.
- ❖ Communicate meaningfully back where necessary.

There is a direct correlation between effective communication and building a meaningful relationship. This also applies to your relationship with Jesus.

<u>**VOICES CALLING...**</u>
There are **many voices in the world** that call out to us to demand our attention. There are voices of deception, lies, twisted truths etc. These voices put us on a wandering path leading us away from the accurate truth of God's Word.

There is **only ONE voice that really matters**, that we should allow to live in our hearts and mind and that is **the voice of God**. That voice calls from the Bible to offer us light and truth. God's Word provides the necessary steadfastness, salvation, and direction we need.
What we hear changes our thinking; changes our lifestyle; it is a matter of life and death based on what we accept or reject and can strengthen our faith.
It is our choice whether we will allow it or not.

<u>**The Modern Church**</u> has strayed from the original accurate message of the Bible as Jesus and the Apostles preached it and has been infected by false doctrines that allow all kinds of circular humanism, opinions and the so called "wisdom" of the world. The result of this is that worldly standards are accepted that is in conflict to the Word of God as found in the Bible; pagan ideas and practices are accommodated in the church and has developed a lukewarm church that results in a powerless church community.

The Original Church of Acts allowed no false dogmatics, regardless of the pressures of the Jews and Gentiles who wanted to introduce their standards into the "new" Church. The Acts Church conveyed to the people a message of truth according to the gospel of Jesus Christ and the principles of the Kingdom of God. It was the same message that Jesus taught. This same message of the Kingdom of God that Jesus conveyed to His disciples, to carry into the world, as apostles, since He sent them forth. It is this message that has brought unity and gave rise to wonders and signs through the working of the Holy Spirit. Read about this in Mark 16:15-18 and Acts 4:23-24,31.

WHERE DID THE IDEA OF APOSTLESHIP COME FROM?

In Luke 6:13 we read:
"Now when the morning came, He called His disciples to Him, and chose twelve of them, **whom He called apostles."**
Notice that it is Jesus who calls the **disciples** and then calls them **Apostles.**
Let's look at the original language's meaning. This is the Greek meaning since the New Testament was originally written in Greek.
The word **"disciples"** is identified in the Strong's Concordance as G3101. The Greek word is "mathetes" and its original meaning is **learner and follower**.
The word **"apostle"** is G652, which in Greek is "apostolos." The original meaning is "**to be set apart (... to God")** and "**he that is sent**" as well as "ambassador of the Gospel of Jesus Christ"

Jesus first taught the disciples how and what to teach the people, and then He sent them as ambassadors/apostles of the gospel of Jesus Christ and the Kingdom of God.

In Hebrews 3:1 we read, "Therefore, holy brethren, partakers of the heavenly calling, **consider the Apostle and High Priest of our confession, Christ Jesus."**
Here we see that Jesus Himself is identified as an Apostle. He was sent by God the Father and did nothing that He didn't hear His Father say or see His Father do.

The Apostles did the same thing. They followed Jesus ' Example.

After Jesus returned to heaven, the **Apostles became the voices of Truth** according to the Gospel of Jesus Christ and the principles of the Kingdom of God.
They were the ambassadors/representatives of Jesus and proclaimed the truth with accuracy and lived it accordingly. They set the example to the people.

It is therefore important to understand the detail of God's Word in accuracy so that we will adhere to accurate truth and faith.

When we study the Bible to hear the voice of God, we can use various methods to discover the truth of God's Word.

NEXT ARE SOME BIBLE STUDY METHODS FOR DISCOVERING THE ACCURATE MESSAGE AND WORD OF TRUTH THAT JESUS REVEALES TO US

If you are serious about seeking and finding the accurate truth of the Word of God in the Bible, it is important not to read the Bible with preconceived ideas, but rather to **read it with an open, a receptive mind.**

The art of reading the Bible is **to read from the Bible** and **NOT** to read **into** the Bible, **which will not reflect the Truth of God accurately.** Considering this, there are two terms that define this reading style.
EISEGESIS is the term used when an additional meaning is read into the text, which does not reflect the original meaning, because the person reading it, has his/her own perception around the passage.

HERMENEUTICS is a method of study that <u>determines the accurate meaning of the Word of God, the Bible.</u> To access the Hebrew and Greek meanings, dictionaries in programs such as having "The Word" or "E-Sword" helps discover the true original meaning and truth of the passage.

Laying down old beliefs and sticking to new ones is not easy, but vital, since Jesus recommended us to abide by His Word and Truth that He has taught. In this way our faith will be purified according to Jesus ' principles.

As we discover the accurate truths, we are confronted with a **NEW LEARNING PROCESS** in which <u>we put off the inaccurate beliefs and accept what is accurate and make it our own,</u> because we know it is a Biblical doctrine and is not human tradition or interpretations. Sometimes it's a sobering, painful process, **but the result of it is pure faith**.

One of the important things to remember here is that we <u>cannot blend the Old Testament doctrines with the New Testament doctrines.</u> Each of the Testaments carry its own message that was appropriate for a specific time. The Old Testament was indeed the shadow of the New Testament, as it pointed in many ways to what was to come, of which the central message was the coming of Jesus Christ, the Messiah, which also was the most important. A good example in the Bible that points out that we cannot blend the Principles and Teachings of the Old and New Testaments is Galatians 4:22-26,30. The sentences in this passage point out a shocking fact, namely, that <u>the message of freedom contained in the New Testament does not apply to the Old Testament lifestyle under the law that spells out bondage.</u> Jesus worked true freedom for us on the cross, so we are no longer under the bondage of law and sin.

Read the Bible from your position in Jesus Christ if you are saved. Without Jesus in your life as a saved child of God, the law of the Old Testament is still in force for you, and you will be judged accordingly. As a saved person, you are free from the law that Jesus fulfilled on your behalf and redeemed you from the punishment you should have received. The latter is part of the New Testament Christian's life.

<u>**PUT EMPHASIS ON DIFFERENT WORDS IN A VERSE AND SEE HOW THE MEANING OF THE VERSE CHANGES AND EXPOSES THE HIDDEN TRUTHS.**</u> Take time and think about the message with each emphasis.

<u>**DETERMINE THE CONTEXT OF THE SCRIPTURE**</u> you are reading. When verses are read out of context, their accurate truth is lost, and wrong messages are passed on to people. The inaccuracy brings deception.

<u>**TOPICAL STUDY IS A HANDY AND EFFECTIVE METHOD**</u> by which one can determine the "golden thread" of God's message in His Word, the Bible. Here you will decide the topic you want to know more about. Software like "E-Sword" and "The Word" help you track down the Scriptures around the topic you're looking at. If you have, for example, decided on a topic such as "firstborn" and ask for a search in Scripture with one of the software programs, it will at least give you about seven Scripture verses about it. After that, you will have to study each passage in context. You will find that the Bible is consistent in the message it carries. Sometimes Scriptures seem to contradict themselves, but with deeper study, you'll find that the verses are affirming and complimenting each other.

<u>**STAY JESUS-CENTERED as you examine His Word/the Bible**</u>. As New Testament Christians, we live with Jesus as the center of our lives. By no means self-centered.

IT IS ALSO NECESSARY TO LOOK AT CONJUNCTIONS, DEFINITIONS, KEYWORDS, AND THE BREAKING UP OF SCRIPTURE IN CHAPTERS AND VERSES.

Conjunctions often connect central thoughts to each other.
Keywords often highlight the important message the Lord wants to bring home to us.
Definitions of words in the Bible are linked to the Hebrew and Greek language and **culture** that will give us better understanding of the passage or subject we are engaged in.
For example, what is the definition of "sin" according to the Bible—what does God mean when He uses that word?
John 1:29 says, "The next day John saw Jesus coming to him, and he said, "There is the Lamb of God who takes away the **sin** of the world!"
The Greek word for "sin" = **"hamartia" (G266)** meaning a sin. The root word in Greek is **"Hamartano" (G264)** which has the following meaning: -
To miss the mark and therefore not to share in the price/ To err/To sin.
It creates an in-depth understanding around sin. Each of us was born with a divine plan for our lives and it is that plan that is the "mark" for our lives. Rather, sinners are not only people who drink liquor, smoke cigarettes, and murder, but are rather those who miss the mark when they are expected to do the will of God. As a result, they forfeit the reward reserved only for obedient children of God.
The **breaking up of Scripture in chapters and verses** was to facilitate its reading, but this resulted in a central message often lost and thus also losing value if it is not read in its fullness.

THERE ARE ALSO SUCH PHENOMENA AS "SHADOWS, TYPES, SYMBOLISM, AND PARABLES" in the Bible that we can examine to better understand what God wants to say to us.
Shadows are often seen in events in the Old Testament that become a reality in the New Testament. For example, the sacrifice of the lamb in the Old Testament was the shadow of Jesus who became our Sacrificial Lamb in the New Testament.
Types can be seen in the life of Joseph who was a type of Jesus who would come in the New Testament.
Symbolism can be seen in the animals sacrificed for men's sins in the Old Testament. The sacrificial animals were symbolic of Jesus sacrificing His life for our sins in the New Testament.
We find **parables** especially in the four Gospels of the New Testament where Jesus used known objects or situations that the people of that time could associate with to convey a specific lesson or message to them.

BACKGROUND OF BIBLE BOOKS ALSO GIVE DEEPER INSIGHT INTO THE EVENTS OF THAT PARTICULAR BIBLE BOOK.
Read Luke 1:1-4 and ask yourself the following questions to identify the background: -
❖ By whom was the Bible book written?
❖ What is the author's motive?
❖ What is the purpose of this book?
❖ In what era/period was the book written?
❖ Read Colossians 4:14 and determine the occupation of the author of the Book of Luke and Acts.

John wrote in John 21:25, "There are many other things that Jesus did. If every one of them were written down, I suppose the whole world would not have room for the books that would be written"

Yes, what a wonderful privilege to be able to hear the voice of God in the Bible as you discover His message in depth and still realize that there are actually many more to discover. His Word is far deeper than we can imagine, yet He wants us to gain insight and wisdom through it, and at the same time learn to understand Him.

There are many precious truths in the Bible
which help you discover how wonderful
the Lord is in all His fullness.
May the journey of discovery through the Bible have
new meaning for you.
May Your relationship with Jesus grow
as He becomes an ever-greater Reality to you.

II. WHEN GOD'S GRACE, MERCY & LOVE FLOWS AS ONE MIGHTY RIVER...

God is Love

The love of God is…
Far beyond human understanding
Greater than what our minds can perceive
Deeper than the deepest heartfelt thoughts
Limitless, without measure
Healing to our spirit, soul, and body.

The love of God…
Surrounds us
like a fresh morning breeze
Drenches us
with every breath we take
refreshes us
 like the early morning dew
yet it is a love closer
than every heartbeat
that our heart takes
Closer than a single secret thought.

The love of God…
How privileged we are!
Rich, amid a poor world
Healing for a Broken Spirit
Closeness to a Lonely Heart
Salvation, forgiveness, redemption
on the cross.

God's Love…
How can we still doubt, wonder, ask?
Is there salvation for me?
Is there a way out…?
of all the pain and heartache?
Is there hope for me in this broken world?

Yes, God's love is meant for you too.
You just must take it in lowliness of heart
Hold it tightly to your heart
Allow it to drench you, too
And enfold you in His Spirit.
And be love for you too.

Written by SE De Jager

WALKING THE PATH OF THE CROSS

Luke 22-24; Luke 9:23,24; John 1:1-4,9-12,14

1 Peter 2:21-24

"For to this you were called, since Christ also suffered for you,
leaving an example for you to follow in His steps.
He committed no sin nor was deceit found in His mouth.
When He was maligned, He did not answer back,
when He suffered, He threatened no retaliation,
but committed Himself to God who judges justly.
He Himself bore our sins in His body on the tree,
that we may cease from sinning and live for righteousness.
By His wounds you were healed.
For you were going astray like sheep
but now you have turned back
to the Shepherd and Guardian of your souls."

A few thousand years ago, there was a heavenly King who willingly exchanged His kingship for a humble, earthly living for the redemption of mankind. This King takes off His royal robe, takes off His crown, and exchanges it all for an ordinary human robe. He takes up an ordinary human status as a carpenter, with His father, in a small town, Nazareth.

No one, except His parents, knew who He really was.

One day He began to tell the people that the Kingdom of God had drawn near, and the King of this kingdom is here on earth. This King came with a special gift of true, perfect love and grace. He heals the sick, cleanses lepers, resurrects the dead, and expels Satan and his wicked spirits from people's lives. He tells wonderful stories (parables) with special messages and life lessons in them. These people can't believe their eyes and ears!

WHO IS HE?

The spiritual leaders get angry, so angry, that they can only think of murder... Why? Because ... This Man, who they think, is so arrogant in His conduct - He proclaims to be God's Son, even God Himself! He "works" on the Sabbath by healing the people! According to their perspective, He is disobedient to the law of God. He tells these spiritual leaders that they are loveless and are leading the nation astray. They have Satan as their father and not God. He proclaims to be the Messiah!

In the room of a house sits this King and His 12 friends, who were His true disciples. They are preparing for supper. Suddenly He gets up, takes a dish of water, and begins to wash His friends' feet. An example of absolute humility and love follows. King Jesus stoops down on His knees to wash dirty, dusty feet! At the end of this humble action, He says to them: "If I then, your Lord and Teacher, have washed your feet, you too ought to wash one another's feet. For I have given you an example – you should do just as I have done for you." John 13:14-15.

One night, on the Mount of Olives, in the garden of Gethsemane, we find Jesus alone, on His knees, distressed with sweat becoming drops of blood. He prays for what He has come to do... In His mind, is a play down of the cruel path that lies ahead. Thoughts of indescribable pain and suffering with a burden of the sin of humankind upon His shoulders that no human can carry... In His struggle He prays, "Father, Your will be done."

In the darkness of the night, Jesus and His disciples hear the rebellious voices of soldiers and people on the way. Like a criminal, Jesus is taken prisoner. He has been betrayed. What a sorrowful sight. The disciples flee and Jesus is left alone in His crisis.

He was brought before the Jewish leaders, King Herod, and eventually before the governor Pontius Pilate.

Jesus is unjustly accused of things He never even did. Jesus never defends Himself. No one comes forward to tell the truth. All of them let Him carry His painful burden and humiliation in solitude. Peter denies that he ever knew Jesus. Even Pilate realized that Jesus was innocent, but that doesn't stop the crowd from killing Him!

King Jesus is mocked, beaten with a whip. His clothes are stripped out and a crown of thorns is brutally pinned to His head. The blood flows over His face and there is no one to help Him. He gets punched with the fist and pushed around. Even His true identity is robbed from Him. Jesus never strikes back. He is so brutally beaten and prosecuted that He can hardly be recognized. This King, who can destroy everyone with one great bolt of lightning, does not!

The blood thirsty crowd screams: "Crucify Him..."

"Pick up your cross and walk!", a soldier shouts, and more whiplash rained down on Jesus' bloodied back. He continues to be driven like an animal. "Today we will put you on another throne!", shouted the soldier. "You're pretending to be a king!"
Jesus stumbles down the streets until He no longer has the strength to do so. His knees give way under Him and he slams down on the gravel road.

"Hey, you, yes, you! Pick up this cross and carry it!" Simon picks up the cross reluctantly and shoulder to shoulder with Jesus, carries the cross to Mount Calvary, the "skull place" of death...

For the people, it was a humiliation to carry this symbol of death. Under the cross on his shoulder, this death burden gets a new meaning to Simon. He doesn't understand well, but after making eye contact with Jesus, he realizes he's doing it for a Man of indescribable love, and it becomes a great honor for him to assist Him in this painful journey. This brief personal contact with Jesus, changes his life for eternity.

Jesus is wildly pushed to the ground and ordered to lie down on the cross.
Jesus' hands and feet are penetrated by nails that are driven in by hammer blows. The pain! The terrible pain! It is our sins, our sicknesses, our sorrow, and brokenness that Jesus carried to the cross and was nailed to the cross with Him! Only a perfect human could pay this indescribable price for humanity. None other, but Jesus who is God in the flesh could pay this ransom.

The cross is lowered into its hole.

This King's body has been crushed for you and me, and His blood flows freely for you and me. The punishment for our sins, are death. In His great love and mercy, Jesus decides to take the death penalty on your and my behalf...

Jesus was not even allowed to remain in His own clothes while He must die! No one really cared. The soldiers argued over Jesus' garments. They divided His clothes, by throughing a dice. In principle, Jesus gives everything up for you and me!

Even while hanging on the cross, Jesus is mocked once again. With the last few breaths that He takes, He says: "Father forgive them for they know not what they do."

3 days later, there is an earthquake, early in the morning, that moves the earth under the soldiers' feet while guarding Jesus' tomb. The stone that was in front of the entrance to Jesus' tomb is rolled away by heavenly forces. And the Soldiers? They chose to run for their lives! In their place two angels await Jesus's followers to give them the good news.

The tomb is empty!! Jesus is risen!!! He has conquered death and sin!!
Only the death robes in which He was covered, remained as a reminder of someone who was once dead.

Something special remains to be seen there. The face cloth that was wrapped around Jesus's face and head was neatly rolled up and left in a place by itself. See John 20:7. Herein lies a very special message. According to Jewish tradition, if the cloth or napkin, is crumpled or not neatly folded, it means that you have finished eating and that the servant can clear and clean the table. **But** if the napkin was folded or rolled up and the man of the house would get up and leave the table, it meant he would come back to eat some more.

With this rolled up face cloth, Jesus is saying to you and me that He is coming back again.

JESUS IS COMING BACK AGAIN. Jesus said the following in John 14:3-4: "And if I go and make ready a place for you, I will come again and take you to be with Me, so that where I am, you may be too. And you know the way where I am going."

Yes, Jesus is coming again to fetch us so that we may live with Him forever. Until then, He will be within us by the presence of His Spirit to guide us in His truth and will. Let us choose to follow in His steps as He guides us with His Spirit and glorify His Name. In this way, Jesus is as close to us as every breath we take....

HALLELUJAH! JESUS IS COMING AGAIN!! ARE YOU READY TO MEET HIM FACE TO FACE?

FOR BY GRACE WE ARE SAVED, THROUGH FAITH, NOT BY OURSELVES NEITHER BY OUR GOOD WORKS, BUT IT IS A GIFT FROM GOD!

Ephesians 2:4-5,8-9
"But God, being rich in mercy, because of His great love with which He loved us, even though we were dead in transgressions, made us alive together with Christ – by grace you are saved!

For by grace, you are saved through faith, and this is not from yourselves, it is the gift of God, it is not from works, so that no one can boast."

Paul speaks in this passage to the converted believers of Ephesus. These people practiced pagan practices before their conversion and had to be taught concerning the Gospel of Jesus Christ and the practical principles of the Kingdom of God.

In Ephesians 2:1-3, Paul explains that when we are unconverted, we are spiritually dead to God but alive to the evil of the world. We live in obedience to Satan and in disobedience to God.

The wonder of this whole hopeless situation is that God's plan of salvation was in place from the beginning, as early as the creation of the earth and in the garden of Eden. Read about it in Genesis 3:15. He had already put it into action in His great mercy and love for us after the fall, even before we were born.

To us as human beings, the matter seems hopeless, but then we see what Ephesians 2:4 begins with... "**BUT GOD...**"
"**BUT GOD, being rich in mercy, because of his great love with which He loved us, even though we were dead in transgressions, made us alive together with Christ – by grace you are saved! –and He raised us up with Him and seated us with Him in the heavenly realms in Christ Jesus, to demonstrate in the coming ages the surpassing wealth of His grace in kindness toward us in Christ Jesus.**" Ephesians 2:4-6.

Yes, the Lord shows up in the most impossible situations to turn it into a spiritual victory!

Let us look deeper than the surface at these verses: -
To see the deeper value, we're going to look at certain words' original meanings.
"**Mercy**" – The Greek word is "**el'-eh-os**" (G1656) – meaning "mercy" with a further meaning of "**divine compassion/tender mercy.**"
"**Love**" – The Greek word in this specific Scripture and context is "**agapē = ag-ah'-pay**" (G26 & G25 with the following original meanings. "Love, **love that is specifically affectionate or benevolence (***well-meaning and kindness***); a love feast (plural): charity.**
"**Grace**" – The Greek word is, "**khar'-ece/charis**" (G5485), it also comes from G5463, and the meaning is further enriched after "**graciousness (as gratifying),** figurative or spiritual; especially **the divine influence upon the heart of man, and its reflection of God's life, in the life of a person;...**

GOD'S CHARACTER IS REVEALED IN THESE VERSES, NAMELY, ...
First of all, **God is love.** This love is full of goodness; It is divine in nature because no human being can truly love someone who rejects him/her and that is exactly what God does. He loved man even before man identified God as his Creator, his God, and Savior. The Lord knew how hopeless man is without salvation, so He reached out through His love, and He gave us an eternal chance for salvation and a new life in Him.

God is merciful towards us. He gives us a new life in Jesus Christ that we do not deserve at all. No, we deserve the punishment of eternal death, **"BUT GOD..."** intervenes for us so we may have the privilege to receive new life that leads to eternal life.

Grace saves you after you obey the message of the truth of Jesus Christ and believe it.
God gives Grace that continually works in a Godly way on our lives and in our hearts.
It is the **divine influence upon the heart of man, and its reflection of God's life, in the life of a person,** that prompts us to accept Jesus as our Redeemer and Savior. Without this constant influence in our lives, we will not be able to grow spiritually.

When we look at Ephesians 2:10, we see that this "salvation package" brings us back to our original divine purpose for which God actually created **us:** -
"For we are His work, created in Christ Jesus for good works, which God prepared beforehand, that **we might walk in them. "**(Meaning that we may do His good works by faith.) It is only possible to live out our unique divine plan for our lives if we choose to walk this path of Salvation in Jesus Christ. That's the starting point because Jesus is making our whole life new.

THE CONFLUENCE OF GRACE, LOVE, AND SALVATION
You and I, and everyone who accepts Jesus as their Lord and Savior, are so privileged to receive forgiveness, be acquitted of the punishment of our sins, and also be saved by God's wonderful grace. God, through Jesus, has given us the greatest gift ever, namely:
- ❖ Freedom in Christ
- ❖ Lasting Peace That Is Unwavering amid trials and troubles
- ❖ A Freedom accompanied by the Deliverance from guilt brought about by sin
- ❖ The Constant Indwelling of His Spirit
- ❖ His Enduring Presence in us
- ❖ His Enduring Protection
- ❖ Eternal life.

"In this is love: not that we have loved God, <u>but that He loved us and sent his Son to be the atoning sacrifice for our sins</u>. No one has seen God at any time. <u>If we love one another, God resides in us, and His love is perfected in us. By this we know that we reside in God and He in us; in that He has given us of His Spirit...</u> If anyone confesses that Jesus is the Son of God, God resides in him and he in God. And we have come to know and to believe the love that God has in us. <u>God is love</u>, and <u>the one who resides in love resides in God, and God resides in him.</u>"**
1 John 4:10,12-13,15-16

HOW DO WE ACCESS GOD'S GRACE?
We read in Romans 5:1-2 **the following: "Therefore, being <u>justified by faith,</u> we** have peace with God through our Lord Jesus Christ; **<u>by whom also THROUGH FAITH WE HAVE GAINED ACCESS TO THIS GRACE in which we stand;</u> and we glory in the hope of the glory of God."** In other words, **<u>OUR FAITH IN THE COMPLETE FULFILLED WORK OF JESUS CHRIST</u> for us** and **mankind, GIVES US ACCESS TO GOD'S GRACE. <u>GRACE IS ACTIVATED BY OUR FAITH IN JESUS CHRIST</u>.**

*Thank you, Abba Father, for your love, grace, and mercy
with which You bless us in abundance.
Thank you for the salvation in Jesus Christ and
Your constant indwelling in our lives.
Thank you for Your constant divine influence in
our hearts and lives
so that we can grow into the child of God
You have planned for us to be.
Help us to fulfill Your divine plan for our lives
for Your glory.
In The Name of Jesus Christ.
Amen.*

"WHAT DO YOU WANT ME TO DO FOR YOU?"

Mark 10:46-52

"They came to Jericho.
As Jesus and His disciples and a large crowd were leaving Jericho,
Bartimaeus the son of Timaeus, a blind beggar, was sitting by the road.
When he heard that it was Jesus the Nazarene, he began to shout,
"Jesus, Son of David, have mercy on me!"
Many scolded him to get him to be quiet, but he shouted all the more,
"Son of David, have mercy on me!"
Jesus stopped and said, "Call him."
So, they called the blind man and said to him, "Have courage! Get up! He is calling you."
He threw off his cloak, jumped up, and came to Jesus.
Then Jesus said to him, "What do you want Me to do for you?"
The blind man replied, "Rabbi, let me see again."
Jesus said to him, "Go, your faith has healed you."
Immediately he regained his sight and followed Him on the road."

Close your eyes for a long period of time and experience the dark darkness that settles on you, listen to everything around you, but don't open your eyes out of curiosity.

From birth, you hear about all the beautiful things about you. People tell you about it and you wish you could see it. What does green, red, blue, and yellow look like and all the other colors everyone is talking about?
Yes, you're blind and know only the black of darkness! Everything around you are just tangible, audible, and you just have to build your own picture in your mind – with only one color, black!

This is the life Bartimaeus lived. No one even wanted to offer him a job. He is "useless" to that time's society, an outcast. Begging is his foreground and "occupation"!

He hears the news from a passerby. There is a wonderful Man who performs many miracles, and everyone wonders if He might be the long-awaited Messiah?! This Man heals the sick and speaks of a particularly unparalleled love and even extends forgiveness to those whom He heals. Bartimaeus wished he could get to meet this Man. Only maybe he'll be able to help him, so he doesn't have to sit in darkness anymore, feeling useless.

Often our lives are just like Bartimaeus's life, even though we are not blind. We are in a spiritual darkness. We live without really knowing Jesus. Our hearts are darkened by various problems, worries, sadness, fears for something and much more. Sometimes this problem, sadness, or whatever it may be, becomes so great that we, only see the darkness in our life, and forget to look for the "Light" that would lead us to the solution we need. It is also often these dark areas in our life that become so big in our minds that it forces us into passivity. We are paralyzed by it, sometimes to the point where we also begin to feel "useless." We lose our hope and faith because we can no longer see Jesus.

One day, the footsteps on the road where Bartimaeus sits are much more than normal. He hears the excited crowd and wonders what's going on. Then he heard it! It's Jesus who is nearby! With new hope and faith, he begins to cry out as loud as he can, crying out to the only hope he has ever had: "Jesus, Son of David, have mercy on me!!!" Repeatedly, he shouts, and when the people try to silence him with the statement that he is not important enough for Jesus to pay attention to Bartimaeus, he just calls out louder and louder.

We also need to take our eyes off our "darkness" and focus on Jesus, who is the light of the world. He is our only hope and true Light in life. It's time for us to call on Him, who knows the answers for all our "darknesses" in our lives. Even if it feels like we are praying against the ceiling, we should continue to pray. Philippians 4:6-7 encourages us with the words: **"Do not be anxious over anything, but in everything by prayer and supplication along with thanksgiving let your petitions be made known to God. And the peace of God, which surpasses all understanding, will guard your hearts and your minds in Christ Jesus."**

Jesus hears his outcry! He asks the people to bring Bartimaeus to Him. Jesus asks him, **<u>"What do you want me to do for you?"</u>**

Do you know that Jesus is standing before you today and specifically asking you, the same question "What do you want me to do for you?" Jesus is in love with you, and he knows your heart. He wants you to share your deepest needs and longings with Him and surrender to Him. He wants to help and bless you today.

"That I may see..." The greatest need this man has ever had! That his darkness will turn into light! We know that Jesus fulfilled this wonderful request with such eternal love for Bartimaeus. Suddenly, Bartimaeus' darkness turned into the most beautiful picture ever — **He sees Jesus!** Jesus, the wonderful Man who turned His darkness into light! An eternal light in his heart and a physical light in his eyes.

Jesus wants your heart's darkness to disappear into His eternal light today. Jesus wants to give you the wonderful gift of His eternal light, His presence in you, through His Spirit. Take your eyes off your problem and focus on Him. Just ask, He is standing in front of you today and saying, **"What do you want me to do for you?"** Take the time to tell Jesus. **Don't let the opportunity pass**. You have His full attention, and He is listening to your deepest need.

"Call unto Me and I will answer you...". says the Lord.

WHEN THE STORMS OF LIFE HIT HARD

James 1:2-4
"My brothers and sisters, consider it nothing but joy
when you fall into all sorts of trials,
because you know that the testing of your faith
produces endurance.
And let endurance have its perfect effect,
so that you will be perfect and complete,
not deficient in anything."

Earlier in the year, a violent storm severely bruised the Sapphire Blue Shower shrub, which grows at my porch, with one main branch. The branch had a greenwood break and lay to the ground. That same afternoon, my husband and I tried to save this injured branch by using some cloth strips and rope to anchor this branch to one of the other stronger branches that were still whole. Together, with the necessary care, we tied this branch to a healthy branch.

Now, months later, I was shoveling in the flower bed to remove some weeds and loosen the soil to enhance growth. To my surprise I could see that the greenwood break had healed, but here was something more to observe. I cut the anchor ropes and rags loose and detached the once injured branch from the healthy branch. Where the break was, a thickened area had formed, strengthening the branch enough to grow on its own. Now this cured branch was firmly anchored to the main trunk. The branch was also the highest of all the branches on this shrub and loaded with flowers!

That's when the Lord reminded me again that we ourselves are often bruised and even broken by the trials of life, but in our commitment to Him, the Great Physician, Comforter, Helper, and Mighty God, we are preserved by Him. He will never leave us nor forsake us, He will not leave us amid the storm, to perish. No, His grip is very firmly on our lives and when we threaten to sink into the depths of the waters of life, it is His hand that rescues us. Jesus plainly assures us in John 10:27-30: **"My sheep** *(the people who believe in Jesus and follow him)* **listen to My voice, and I know them, and they follow Me. I give them eternal life, and they will never perish, and no one will snatch them out of My hand. My Father, which gave them to Me, is greater than all; And no one can snatch them out of My Father's hand. "The Father and I are one."**

God is inseparably connected to us, and His love is enduring. In Him lies our strength when we feel too weak to move on. It sometimes takes months to fully experience the inner healing that our Great Physician, Jesus, is working for us, but it is at this time that the Lord makes the necessary changes in our lives. It's painful but necessary. That which is not complementary to our lives and not contributing to His glory, is removed, and replaced with new life-giving Holy Spirit inspired qualities that bring growth and adorn our lives, like the beautiful flowers on this shrub. It is the Holy Spirit's powerful qualities that adorn our lives, to the glory of our Abba Father.

When our healing is completed and we walk in His freedom, we are still securely anchored in Him, just as the branch is anchored to the main trunk. It is from this attachment that the life-giving food comes, that keeps the branch strong and healthy. Jesus said in John 15:4-5: **"Remain** *(abide)* **in Me, and I will remain** *(abide)* **in you. Just as the branch cannot bear fruit by itself, unless it remains in the vine, so neither can you unless you remain in Me. I am the vine; you are the branches. The one who remains in Me – and I in him – bears much fruit, because apart from Me you can accomplish nothing."**

We need to be nourished by Jesus too, so that amid this stormy life, we can be strong enough to resist the spiritual attack.

Therefore, we must watch and pray and continually drench our lives with His Word, so that regardless of seasons we will blossom to the glory of our Abba Father.

Thank you, Abba Father,
for your strong grip on my life...
Thank you for holding me tight and
being anchored in You...
Thank you that I can trust You
for a perfect healing and
that I may know that You
will make my life blossom in your Spirit,
for Your glory.
Grant that my life will spread
the sweet aroma of Jesus' love...
In Jesus' Name Alone
Amen

THE CHARACTER OF THE GOOD SAMARITAN - WHO DID HE REPRESENT?

Luke 10:27-37
"Now an expert in religious law stood up to test Jesus, saying,
"Teacher, what must I do to inherit eternal life?"
He said to him, "What is written in the law? How do you understand it?"
The expert answered, "Love the Lord your God with all your heart, with all your soul,
with all your strength, and with all your mind, and love your neighbor as yourself."
Jesus said to him, "You have answered correctly; do this, and you will live."
But the expert, wanting to justify himself, said to Jesus
"And who is my neighbor?"
Jesus replied, "A man was going down from Jerusalem to Jericho, and
fell into the hands of robbers, who stripped him, beat him up, and went off,
leaving him half dead.
Now by chance a priest was going down that road, but when he saw the injured man,
he passed by on the other side.
So too a Levite, when he came up to the place and saw him,
passed by on the other side.
But a Samaritan who was traveling came to where the injured man was,
and when he saw him, he felt compassion for him.
He went up to him and bandaged his wounds, pouring oil and wine on them.
Then he put him on his own animal, brought him to an inn, and took care of him.
The next day he took out two silver coins and gave them to the innkeeper, saying,
'Take care of him, and whatever else you spend,
I will repay you when I come back this way.'
Which of these three do you think became a neighbor to the man
who fell into the hands of the robbers?"
The expert in religious law said, "The one who showed mercy to him."
So, Jesus said to him, "Go and do the same."

Luke 10 begins with Jesus' teaching and sending out the disciples and seventy others with a mission, a message and divine task that equips them for their divine task.

It is remarkable that the Good Samaritan's story is told in the same chapter. I believe God leaves nothing to chance. He has good reason for everything. There is a deeper meaning in this story that Jesus told the church leaders that were well acquainted with the law. It is a meaning that relates to our relationship with our Heavenly Father. Being a child of God, or being a disciple of Jesus, is more than just doing all the right things. **1 John 4:17b says "... As He is, so are you in this world."** What is the secret and connection of this verse and the story of the Good Samaritan?

The story of the Good Samaritan reflects a "scene" from our everyday lives. One that we don't like very much, but that will always be there until the coming of Jesus.

Two people with important status, highly placed "church leaders," a priest and Levite, come the same way, as where a typical predatory scene played itself out a few hours ago. The robbers had no mercy. The man was robbed from head to toe and then beaten half-dead and left by the side of the road in anticipation of his final death sentence... Ironically, these two important church leaders turn their heads away as the man's faint cry for help rings in their ears. They distance themselves from the man in need.

In their hearts they reason with the voice of the Holy Spirit, encouraging them to help, but with words such as "not now, Lord, I'm too busy, I don't have the time now, I'm going to be late for the church service where I'm going to worship You, what am I going to look like if I have to work with the bloodied body now and who says this man is not just pretending and plan to attack ME?!! No, just not now, what are the people going to think of me when I pay attention to the dirty old beggar? He'll be here again, next time I pass by!"

... But life goes on and someone else comes along the same path. One who has been greatly rejected, despised, and counted as a round "0"—a Samaritan! (The Jews have no time, for him because he is a hybrid brood, the offspring among a bunch of stupid Jews who have become mixed with the Assyrians.) Yet this Samaritan had qualities in His character that were lacking in so many other people. This man who is counted as a nothing by the world becomes a love tool in God's hands. Someone who was willing to listen to the voice of the Holy Spirit in his heart and allow God to touch and change the lives of others through him. He fits in the description Paul gives in 1 Corinthians 1:26-28.

BASED ON THE SAMARITAN'S ATTITUDE, WE BEGIN TO SEE JESUS' IMAGE AND ATTITUDE: -

Verse 33 says: "**... and when he saw him....**" He looked much deeper than the surface.
As an outsider, he could also have reasoned that he was too hasty, too busy, and already dressed for his appointment; that this man may well be drunk and does not bother to find a job, just beg for the hard -earned money of others to waste it out again.... Anyway, how will he know now if it's not just a smart set to rob someone? No, the Samaritan allows the Holy Spirit to show him a deeper picture, the one God wants him to see. This man was robbed, physically destroyed, and left for dead. Satan makes sure that we fall deep enough into sin, that he can rob us not only physically but also spiritually and emotionally. His final stab is real eternal death.

Verse 33 tells us that the Samaritan felt **"pity" for the man**. He had genuine compassion. The Samaritan's heart was sincere, full of compassion, willing to stop at a man who could no longer bear his own painful burden. He was willing to help carry his burden in life and also fulfill the love law of Christ. Read of it in Galatians 6:2. It is this heart attitude that drove the Samaritan to true action!

Verse 34 says that "**... "After he went..."** With legs of grace and mercy... He steps up to where the crisis is, kneeling to the level of the man in need, serving him with the grace of healing and divine love. It's love in practice. It requires a humble heart to stoop down, bow down, or kneel, where the crisis level is. Isaiah 42:3 reminds us that Jesus does not extinguish the wick of the faint, smoking lamp or break the crushed reed, no, it is Jesus' Divine Light that shines into the broken world right into the crisis bringing relief and healing; It is Jesus who restores, frees, strengthens, and equips the broken, the crushed reeds, and equips them with the gift of His Spirit.

Like Jesus, this Samaritan was willing to do the **"kneeling."** When was the last time you and I seriously interceded for someone in need? Are you praying for someone who is lost to God's kingdom?

The Samaritan **"bound up his wounds and poured oil and wine on them."** As verse 34 says. His caring hands are instrumental to the guidance and working of the Holy Spirit in this man's life. It is Jesus who works from within us to produce healing and gives new life. In Psalm 147:3 we see that it is God who heals us when we are broken and who binds up our wounds. It was part of the commission Jesus gave to His disciples — **cleansing, healing, and delivering....**

Read Matthew 10:8 and Luke 10:9 on this. It is worth noting that sickness is often associated with our sinful condition. When we decide to stop the practice of sin in our lives, confess it, and ask for forgiveness, we can expect to receive divine healing in spirit, soul, and body. See Psalm 103:3 & James 5: 14b,15,16. When God has done this for us, it is time to become a vessel of His healing of spirit, soul, and body, in dependence on Jesus, by ministering His Word in truth to people.

Verses 33 & 34 depict a further outstanding character trait of this Samaritan. **He was willing to sacrifice time, comfort, and money for this man in need.** He interrupts his journey that had a planned destination, he sacrifices his comfort to ride on his donkey, for the man, by having him ride on his donkey, and pays the inn costs for the man's stay and care. The Samaritan was not self-centered, within his own busy world, but rather remained Jesus-centered, sensitive to His Spirit so that he could do, in spiritual obedience, what God wanted him to do.

How busy is our schedules in life? Has it become too busy to make time for God? Perhaps too busy to look deeper than the surface, too afraid to notice those in need and offer a helping hand or to perform a caring act?

Verse 35 tells us that the Samaritan's care also included **aftercare.** The Samaritan not only helped the man through his crisis but made sure that he could handle his "new" life. He goes away to reach his destination but ensures that the injured man will be followed up with the necessary care. The Samaritan was willing to take responsibility for the full aftercare as well. He looked deeper than the surface once again, so that the man would be assured of a good future. So often we help people only halfway and once the person seems to be taking a few shaky steps in the right direction, we withdraw and forget about the person. Long-standing wrong, sinful habits aren't changed in an instant, or even in a few weeks or months. It is a systematic process that includes spiritual struggles and victories to get such a person back to living God's principles. It is our responsibility to help one another to remain steadfast in the Lord.

Jesus sacrificed His all to give us free access on the path of righteousness that ends with eternal life with Him as John 3:16 proclaims. Jesus paid for us with His life. He also did the aftercare in that He gave His Spirit to help us, sustain us, comfort us, guide us, teach us in every facet of our existence. Please read John 14:16,17,26 & John 15:26 as well as John 16:7-13 on this matter. Jesus also promised that He would come back to fetch us to be with Him. See John 14:1-3.

WHO IS THE BEREAVED, BROKEN, INJURED HALF-DEAD MAN WHO LIES SOMEWHERE ON YOUR LIFE PATH?
Satan and the practices of sin rob us of God's joy and prosperity. This leads to many mental and emotional and even physical wounds. The profound consequences of sin separate us from the eternal, loving presence of our heavenly Father as we progressively die spiritually. It is only the grace of God that works in a willing heart of a disciple/apostle who can work the healing of this broken victim. Galatians 6:9-10 reminds us, **"Let us not grow weary of doing good, for in due season we shall reap if we do not give up. So then, while we have the opportunity, let us do good to all..."**

WHO IS MY NEIGHBOR?
Notice the question Jesus asks the expert in religious law in Luke 10:36: **"Which of these three, do you think, was the neighbor of him who fell among the robbers?"**

To understand the full meaning of "neighbor" within context of the Old and New Testaments, we need to look at what the perception of that time was.

In the **Old Testament,** we see various passages of Scripture such as Exodus 2:11-13 where "brothers" are spoken of respectively as fellow believers/fellow Hebrews and who were therefore seen as his/her neighbor, in this case, they were Moses' neighbor. It is further defined in the original writings in reference H7453 where it is defined as "associates"/"friend, brother".

In verse 13 we see Moses asking the Hebrews why they fight with one another while they are each other's "neighbor." Here we see that "neighbor" in Hebrew in the reference H7453 conveys the same concept, as "neighbor/fellow man/ fellow Hebrew".

Other Scriptures in this regard are found in Leviticus 25:14 and Leviticus 19:17. The latter passage defines "neighbor" in the original Hebrew in H5997 as "companion/fellow neighbor/kindred man – brother." It gives the perspective that your "neighbor" in the Old Testament context is linked to your fellow compatriot and or your family members. These are people who are close to you who you should treat well and not oppress.

JESUS CREATES A NEW PERSPECTIVE, ON WHO MY NEIGHBOR IS, IN THE NEW TESTAMENT.
In Luke 10:27 & 37, "neighbor" in the Greek language in G4139 is defined as "plesion" which means "close by, near neighbor, that is fellow Christian, friend."

Jesus asks from the perspective of **the injured man's position who his neighbor** is.
For the expert in religious law, answering this question, was in principle a difficult since it was the Samaritan. The one person they abhorred, and they also considered themselves superior to the Samaritans.

The Samaritan did good to the injured man who was on his way from Jerusalem to Jericho. There is a possibility that this man was in actual fact a Jew of origin. For the Samaritan, this would mean that he was an "enemy" based on the poor attitude and relations between the two national groups. Yet we see this Samaritan practicing and living out Divine Love in Practice.

In John 5:38-42, Jesus once again speaks to the Jews and experts of religious law. Verse 42 tells us that they don't have the love of God in them. In verse 38, He also points out that they do not have the word and truth of Jesus enduring in them, because they do not believe that it is God the Father who sent Him. These are shocking realities of that time period's circumstances.

In Romans 5:5, Paul says that **the love of God is poured out in our hearts by the Holy Spirit**. This is very good news, because the love of God is in our midst, and we have the freedom to practice it. Moreover, as children of God, He is dwelling in us through His Spirit and God is love!! So, if we should submit to the guidance of the Holy Spirit, He will demonstrate God's love from within us outwardly for the world to see and experience.

1 John 2:5-6 declares our identity in Christ Jesus through the love of God within us, when he says: **"But whoever obeys His word, truly in this person the love of God has been perfected. By this we know that we are in Him. The one who says he resides in God ought himself to walk just as Jesus walked."**

In the **New Testament**, we see further that our brothers and sisters in Jesus are our neighbors according to the definition we have considered here. **Jesus says that His brothers and sisters are the ones who do the will of His Father. This perspective makes your "neighbor" not only your fellow people or biological family, but everyone, regardless of their origin, doing the will of Abba Father.** Read about it in Matthew 12:50.

At the same time, we see **Jesus advising us to love our enemies, bless them, and do good to those who hate you, according to Matthew 5:43-48.** Is it easy, definitely not?! Only in God's power and love this is possible.

Jesus qualifies not only who your neighbor is, in His parable, but also the fact that, you need to do good to those whom you consider to be your enemy.

<u>**WHAT POSITION ARE YOU IN TODAY?**</u>
<u>**Are you the man who was robbed and left to die of his injuries or are you the Samaritan?**</u>

If you may be the robbed, broken, and injured man, remember that your brokenness can be healed and often become instrumental in the hands of the Lord. Psalm 51:17 says, "**The sacrifices of God are a broken spirit. A broken and contrite heart, o God, You will not despise (reject).**" It is amid our brokenness that we become useful to God. If you have nothing but the pieces of your broken life today to present to God, you are in the right place. Pick up those pieces in your spirit and offer them to Him. It is He who heals, it is He who delivers us, who binds our wounds and makes us a new creation. Read 1 Corinthians 5:17.

When we cleanse ourselves of all the wrong things in our lives and allow Jesus' blood to wash us clean, we become a vessel of honor, useful in God's hands! 2 Timothy 2:20,21 explains it this way: "But in a great (wealthy) house there are not only vessels of gold and of silver, but also of wood and of earth; and some to honor, and some to dishonor. If a man therefore purge (cleanses) himself from these, he shall be a vessel unto honor, sanctified (set apart), and useful for the master's use, and prepared unto every good work."

 It is those who are considered nothing in the world that God finds so precious that He uses them to be vessels of honor to Him in this world, as defined in <u>1 Corinthians 1:26-30</u> which says the following: "**Think about the circumstances of your call, brothers and sisters. Not many were wise by human standards, not many were powerful, not many were born to a privileged position. But God chose what the world thinks foolish to shame the wise, and God chose what the world thinks weak to shame the strong. God chose what is low and despised in the world, what is regarded as nothing, to set aside what is regarded as something, so that no one can boast in his presence. He is the reason you have a relationship with Christ Jesus, who became for us wisdom from God, and righteousness and sanctification and redemption, so that, as it is written, "Let the one who boasts, boast in the Lord."**

Galatians 6:9-10 reminds us, "**Let us not tire out in doing good, for in due season we shall reap if we do not give up. So then, while we have the opportunity, let us do good to all...**"

Choose today to draw near to God and allow Him to sort out your life. "Draw close to God and He will draw close to you", says James 4:8. He can put all the pieces of your life back in place, because His grace is sufficient for you and in your weakness His power is accomplished. See 2 Corinthians 12:9,10.

Your experience of brokenness often becomes your testimony to the Lord with which you can pick others up and lead them to Jesus. You can also become someone's neighbor, led by God's Spirit in you. You can become a servant of mercy.

" For even hereunto were you called:
because Christ also suffered for us,
leaving us an example, that you should follow in His steps"
1 Peter 2:21.

THE BENT WOMAN, THE CHURCH AND YOU...

Luke 13:10-17

"Now He (Jesus) was teaching in one of the synagogues on the Sabbath,
and a woman was there who had been disabled by a spirit for eighteen years.
She was bent over and could not straighten herself up completely.
When Jesus saw her, He called her to Him and said,
"Woman, you are freed from your infirmity."
Then He placed His hands on her, and
immediately she straightened up and praised God."

We are visiting the temple today. There we find Jesus again. He is so busy with everyone around Him, but not too busy to see a particular little woman among the people.

For 18 years she has been suffering from a progressive illness that has already bent her body over so that she can no longer walk upright at all. The Bible tells us that it was an evil spirit of infirmity that caused this disease. She is so badly bent over that she can only look to the ground and behind herself, between her legs. All she sees are the feet of the people around her and the ground at her own feet... The sun in the blue sky, the green of the fields and plants around her, is far beyond her field of vision these days. It's too painful to look up and she has given up on trying. Having a vision for the future? No, it is no longer part of her frame of reference. She shuffles her feet slowly in an effort to move where she wants to be. Today she just longs to be in God's presence, here in the temple. That's all that matters to her.

Often our hearts, like this woman's physical appearance, are crooked and bent over due to worries and pains of life. The burdens of life are bending us over as it becomes heavier and bigger. Our vision for the future is also distorted by this and progressively we live a life with no positive vision for the future. We forget about the once wonderful times with Jesus, when we were visited by Him at the special quality times, we spent with Him. Some of us have not even yet thought about giving Jesus a chance in our lives. Life goes on racing onwards and we are swept away by it. The burdens and problems make us powerless to seek a solution because it has become all we can see. We are so tired of all the questions, and we no longer know if this heavy load will ever get lighter again. We have long forgotten the divine invitation: **"Cast all your worries upon Him, for He cares for you."** As written in 1 Peter 5:7.

Jesus calls this woman to Him. Today, her moment with Jesus has arrived! She moved closer to Jesus' feet. Jesus lays His hands on her, and He says, " "Woman, you are freed from your infirmity." Suddenly, all the muscles begin to loosen up and the bone structure of this bent woman becomes strong, healthy, and upright again! It's a glorious miracle that no one expected! She looks up in Jesus' face and can't help but leap for joy and sing praises to the Lord! She was delivered. She is healthy. She has reason to praise and glorify God!

Jesus wants to take the burden that leaves you so bent over and without any future vision on His own shoulders. He says to you today: **"Come to me, all you who labor and are heavy burdened, and I will give you rest!"** What makes your heart so crooked and bent over today? Have you ever lost all hope that He will ever deliver you from this crooked heart? Jesus sees you and listens to your heart and He hears your cry. He is still our true Physician today. Nothing is impossible for Him; we just need to have faith in Him.

Let us look deeper into this event, and seek to find the mysteries of what God also wants to convey to us through His Word...

THE SYMBOLISM AND DEEPER MEANING...

This **event plays out within the church/synagogue and creates the background for a deeper meaning.** When one looks at the **symbolic meaning of "woman" in** the Bible, especially in the New Testament, we find that it represents church/church goers/church leaders/people of faith.

A spirit of illness and infirmity is a type of dogma within the church community, which in this case represents heresy. It is a progressive process that takes the church's focus away from Jesus, changing the focus on worldly practices and deception. Dogma begins to turn its focus on how to attract and please people than to glorify Jesus.

The **disease** is similar to something like Osteoporosis or in very severe cases Ankylosis which is a degenerative process of particularly the bone structure, which drastically restricts movement and if left untreated, can pull the person/woman very crooked and bent over to the extent that he/she will have to look between their legs to walk or just have ground vision. This means that the person/woman will have to **walk backwards** to get somewhere. The backward movement has become the way to move forward for her!

The church (symbolically the woman) operates on a dogma based on the **"Preceding Word"** and NOT on the **"Proceeding Word"**. "Preceding Word" represents for example the Old Testament lifestyle that is usually very legalistic in nature, as was practiced in the synagogues by the legalistic religious leaders. They were not at all receptive to the new **"Proceeding Word" of Jesus' Gospel**. We also see this in the response to the healing that took place, here in Luke 13. Look at verses 14-16.

The worst malformation of the disease (dogma/heresy) is **around the waist of the person/woman's body which is weakened and can no longer provide support** for the person/woman to walk upright. **This deformation of apostolic truth that includes the gospel of the Kingdom of heaven and of Jesus Christ has the same impact on the modern church today. This made the church powerless.** Why? Because the Truth of the Gospel of Jesus Christ and the Principles of the Kingdom of God is not preached accurately anymore. Thus, our spiritual armor of God, as described in Ephesians 6:14 and Acts 12:8, which includes **the Belt of Truth, has fallen off and is not active as it should be. It is this belt that keeps all the other armor equipment in position.**

When the church is caught up in false dogma and heresy that is not in line with God's Word and Truths, especially concerning the Gospel of Jesus Christ and the principles of the Kingdom of God, they basically carry the spiritual Armor "upside down!" That means, the Breastplate of Righteousness is also "upside down." This could mean that such a church does not preach righteousness by faith but rather by good works and legalism. Moreover, the Belt of Truth has fallen off which means that the person appears naked in the spirit, because the clothing kept in place with the belt of Truth cannot remain in place. Nothing can stay as a covering since the Belt of Truth is the center and anchor of the armor garment and equipment. Jesus warns us in Revelation 16:15 with these words: **"Look! I will come like a thief! Blessed is the one who stays alert and does not lose his clothes so that he will not have to walk around naked, and his shameful condition be seen."** Refresh your memory again because of what Jesus said to the congregation of Laodicea because of their clothing in Revelation 3:17&18.

The woman's head is practically against the earth, indicating that fleshly thinking and disposition within the church are more of a priority than having Kingdom thinking and a disposition according to the Gospel of Jesus Christ is also at hand. In such cases, it is all about a humanistic ideology and satisfying the people's needs. The focus is no longer focused on Jesus and on His will and to honor Him. The church activities are virtually no different from worldly practices.

We can ask ourselves — what or who is the modern church clinging to, today?

1 Corinthians 6:17 says: **"But the one united with the Lord is one spirit with Him".** In other words, the opposite is also true, that if we introduce pagan worldly practices into the church, we are one spirit with the world and the evil one. Should believers adhere to this dogma, which is not the pure Apostolic truths that represents the Gospel of Jesus Christ and the Kingdom of heaven, they are one spirit with the world. This is what Paul says, among other things. Read more about it in 1 Corinthians 6:15,16 and in 1 Thessalonians 4:3,7,8.

If you should stand upright, just like this woman after she was touched and healed by Jesus, a heavenly thinking according to the Gospel of Jesus and the Kingdom of heaven principles, has come to full effect, like a healthy New Testament Church, as described in Acts. The body or congregation has been healed. Read about it in Acts 2:42-47.

This woman is in the synagogue where the **Old Testament message, that is, "Preceding Word,"** which includes righteousness according to works of the law, is preached. The Helmet of Salvation is also "upside down" as the woman/church is in a bent position. It is symbolic of the salvation sought by animal sacrifices and works of "righteousness" according to the law. These modern-day churches include, among others, the following practices and religions that contain "upside down" spiritual perceptions and beliefs that oppose the doctrine of Jesus Christ. These include Legalism, Human/cultural traditions, Humanism, Secularism, "Churchism" – Institution directed and all kinds of fleshly attitudes. This reverse thinking is also spelled out in Romans 1:28-32 in opposition to the knowledge of the Truth that comes from God.

This includes, among others, the following concepts:

These people "do not recognize God" (verses 18-19,28) – The Greek meaning for "acknowledgement/to acknowledge" is found in G2192, which denotes to **"echo."** In other words, **they do not "echo" God's doctrine of truth.** They follow their own thinking, and, in the process, they play God and put themselves above God.

God "gave them up" (v. 24) – or "gave them over..." The Greek word used here, we find in G3860 = "paradydomi" meaning **"to surrender" or "to entrust".** These people choose whom they want to serve. God allowed them to surrender to themselves and their evil conduct.

Notice that verse 25 further **spells** out the attitude of these people. They are those who did not honor and serve God but chose the living creatures over and above the Creator who is to be praised forever. This fact is further defined in verse 28"And because **they did not consider it worth keeping God in recognition, God gave them over to a bad attitude to do what was not appropriate."** The word **"attitude" is also indicative of thoughts**. These people no longer have an accurate doctrine of God, **but their own ideas and their own thinking. They do not "echo" God's truth. "Bad attitude"** in Greek, we find in G96 = "adocimos" which means **"unapproved, worthless and rejected."** To join it, with mind/thoughts, we see that "mind" in G3563 = "nooce" meaning **"intellect" feeling, will and understanding**. In the context of verse 28, we see worldly thinking and doing that is not appropriate. The sad thing about this matter is that God has revealed Himself to these people and so they have knowledge of Him but choose to turn their backs on Him.

Fleshly thinking also includes belief in the mystical things, illusions, superstitions, illogical thinking, "damaged thinking" due to life events and experiences, adherence to traditions, suspicion self-justification, vindictiveness, inferiority, critical thinking and attitude towards others and pride etc. **Each of these above things and attitudes oppose the Truths of God and His kingdom and blocks you from living in His accurate truth.**

Remember: "Accurate doctrine results in accurate conduct."

Thus, bad attitudes involve the fleshly worldly dogma, resulting in the aligned conduct.
We need the attitude and thinking of Jesus Christ. This is only possible when we maintain a living relationship with Him by taking time to study His Word and allow His Spirit to reveal and interpret it to us. When you are raised up into an upright position by the Gospel of Jesus Christ, you begin to live in the accurate truth of His Word so that our mind and perceptions are renewed as we live in godliness.

If you are in a bent position, for example, and you are looking at a "9" you'll see a "6." That's the number that represents humankind/people.
If you looked at the "9" from an upright position, you would see the true number "9". The number **"9" represents and speaks of "Divine Completeness" that can only be obtained living in alignment with the accurate truth of Jesus Christ's Gospel and the Kingdom of heaven's principles.**

Your perception determines your outlook, and
your outlook determines your code of conduct.
Make sure your perceptions are according to God's Truth,
because then your code of conduct will "echo God's Truth."

YOU AND GOD'S VALUE SYSTEM

Psalm 139:14
"I will praise Thee,
for I am fearfully and wonderfully made:
marvelous are Thy works; and that my soul knows right (very) well."

Life can be a terrible negative place. Many people experience this negativity already from birth or even before birth when the parents experience an unwanted pregnancy. The unborn baby experiences this as rejection — that my parents don't want me and so this child doesn't feel loved.

If you have been spared this trauma, you will be able to remember as far as your childhood how negatively the world can sometimes handle a person: -
➤ From an early age, a person is confronted by, for example a teacher who turns your school life into a nightmare or children who bully you physically or verbally.
➤ Sometimes the negativity can grip a person right inside your home, via your spouse or other family.
➤ The workplace also often becomes a place of negativity when your boss or fellow colleagues dislike, abuse, insult or never acknowledge you.
➤ Sometimes we are faced with unemployment that is extremely demoralizing.
➤ I also don't know of a newspaper that predominantly reports any positive news. It's usually all the damning, negative news from other people and events.
➤ Then there are world circumstances that change drastically due to profound events such as COVID 19 that so easily put you in a sense of hopelessness and make you wonder if there will ever be a prosperous future again.

You can list many other examples within your circumstances or people you encounter. It is this negativity that can bring profound consequences to one's human dignity, such as low self-esteem, dissatisfaction, frustration, and heaps of stress. These consequences take its toll on your interpersonal relationships, even on those whom you love and are dear to you.

We need **to remind ourselves regularly that God has a different value system, according to which He judges us.**

From the beginning of creation, we see that God has nurtured positive thoughts about you and me.
In Genesis 1:26 and Genesis 2:20-22, we read that God created man in His own image. Have you ever thought deeply about this? **You were created in God's image!** This is a breathtaking fact! The more important part is that God has revealed Himself as a God and Father of family right from the beginning. In Luke 3:38 we see **Adam as the first created son of God, meaning that God is Adam's Father**. Every human being has the opportunity to become a child of God through the process of being born again.

You don't have to feel inferior at all or feel that your existence is a mistake. God doesn't create a mess! He had a unique plan and purpose in mind just for you, the day He created you. Only you can fulfill that divine plan. He is the only living God who can create perfectly. Everything He creates is good and right and fits perfectly into life as He planned it to be.

In Jeremiah 29:11-14 God says to Israel, but also to you and me: -
"For I know what I have planned for you,' says the LORD. 'I have plans to prosper you, not to harm you. I have plans to give you a future filled with hope.
When you call out to Me and come to Me in prayer, I will hear your prayers. When you seek Me in prayer and worship, you will find Me available to you. If you seek Me with all your heart and soul, I will make myself available to you,' says the LORD."

Although this prophecy is addressed to Israel, it also reveals God's character toward the people He created and loves us. No one can ever tell you again that your future looks bleak and that you are heading for disaster just because he/she thinks you are a failure! When you are God's child, believing and trusting in Him, you know with all certainty that your future is in His hands and that He will work all things together for your good and for His glory. See what Romans 8:28 says. He invites you to be in a living love relationship with Him through prayer and worship.

 As a true child of God, you are in the privileged position of being part of Abraham's offspring from a spiritual perspective. We read of this in Galatians 3: 26,27,29, which says: "For **you are all children of God through faith in Christ Jesus, because all of you who have been baptized into Christ have put on Christ. And if ye be Christ's, then are ye Abraham's seed, and heirs according to the promise."**
Here we find an important key to being a child of God. **Faith!** We know that Abraham was the father of faith and that he was justified by faith. His offspring included physical Israel and now also spiritual Israel.

God's love for you and me is so great that even sin couldn't keep God from wanting an active relationship with us!
Jesus declares to Nicodemus in John 3:16: **"For God so loved the world, that He gave His only begotten Son, that whoever believes in Him should not perish but have everlasting life."**

Through Christ Jesus, God opened the way for us to tear down the wall of sin so that we can stand in the right relationship with Him. God gives us an opportunity to be born again, not from a natural process, but a divine process that only He can work in us. Please read John 3:3,5, and Ephesians 2:14.
He considers us, as human beings, so precious that He designed a "method" by which we can be united with Him in a love relationship: -

❖ When we heed to the voice of the Holy Spirit that convicts us of sin, judgment, and righteousness as described in John 16:8-11,13 and accept Jesus by inviting Him into our lives and making Him King of our heart, we are reborn of divine seed in Spirit and in truth of the Word.

❖ Our spirit is made new through the working of the Holy Spirit, having been cleansed by the blood of Jesus and receiving forgiveness. See John 3:5 & 1 John 1:7,9.

❖ **1 Peter 1:22-23** says, " You have purified your souls by obeying the truth to show sincere mutual love. So, love one another earnestly from a pure heart. **You have been born anew, not from perishable but from imperishable seed, through the living and enduring Word of God."** This fact is further confirmed in 1 John 3:9-10.

❖ During this whole event in your spiritual life, God, through His Spirit, comes into your life, resulting in the fruit of the Spirit and a walk with the Holy Spirit.

❖ You are born new into God's family which also makes you an heir with Jesus, thereby gaining eternal life in God's kingdom. See Romans 8:16,17. God wants us to become His sons and daughters so that He can be our Father. Read about it in 2 Corinthians 6:18.

❖ Do you know that you are part of a royal family? Yes, You are part of a royal family! It doesn't sound like a failure to me, waiting to happen!

Now we are measured against a new value system

1 Petrus 2:9 says: "But you are a <u>chosen race, a royal priesthood, a holy nation, a people of His own</u>, so that you may proclaim the virtues of the One who called you out of darkness into his marvelous light."

You are: -

❖ **Part of a chosen race/generation** — Part of God's chosen nation — Being chosen means that God knows your name and has chosen you specifically. Isaiah 43:1b. you are set apart unto Him.

❖ **Royal.** As you've seen before, your part of a royal family. Your identity is linked to God's family. Also see 2 Corinthians 6:18 & Romans 8:16,17.

❖ **Priesthood.** Do you realize that if God tells you that you have this quality, you actually have access with Jesus into the Most Holy place, where God sits on His throne of grace? You have access to God's holy presence. How can you enter into that special holy place? Through your worship and prayer in your secret closet. Hebrews 4:14-16.

❖ **Holy.** This means that God looks at you through Jesus Christ who cleansed you with His blood so that you can be holy and acceptable to God. Holy also means that you <u>are set apart for God alone</u> and therefore cannot be shared with something else or someone else. See Peter 1:15,16.

❖ You are **His own**. God blessess you as His own. This gives you and me a sense of belonging.

❖ **God called you out of darkness into His light.** Do you remember? He knows you by name, and yet your name is engraved on His palm so that He will not forget you. Read Isaiah 49:15,16.

Praise the Lord for His goodness, grace, and endless love! Without Him, we would never have been able to gain this status! We can rightly declare I am the King's child! My Father is the King of the Universe! This status God gives us as an act of His grace and love for us. We could not earn it at all.

Along with this value system comes a new responsibility that includes:

❖ To grow spiritually and to pursue sanctification. See 1 Peter 2:1,2,3.

❖ We are called to follow in Jesus' footsteps, by living in obedience to God's will for us. Read 1 Peter 2:21.

❖ To witness how we have been saved from our dark, sinful life and brought into God's Light, testifying of God's divine influence in our lives. 1 Peter 2:9.

❖ We are called to a life of praise and worship to God. Read about it in 1 Peter 2:9 Hebrews 13:15 & Ephesians 1:5,6,12.

Mercifully, God does not leave us to do so in our own strength but equips us with the power of His Spirit. Read about this in John 16:13 & Ephesians 1:17,18 & 1 John 2:27. The Holy Spirit is our Teacher and reveals to us the mysteries of God when we are in relationship with Him.

What we need to understand very clearly is that **being a child of God is a progressive process**. We "**grow**" into the position, like a child who systematically reaches adulthood. Notice what John 1:12 tells us about this: **"But as many as received Him, to them He gave the right to become God's children, to those who believe in His Name."**

Choose to be part of God's family, follow in Jesus' footsteps, and be sensitive to the voice of His Spirit. In all of this lies the secret of true life, true peace, true joy, and the opportunity to remain in God's presence all the time.

You are right in the center of God's love.
You are so indescribably close to His heart
because He carries you against His breast.
Do you remember?
You are even carried by Him in this moment.
He can and will not forget you.
Your name is engraved in His palm!

"*I DO NOT CONDEMN ANYONE, NOW...*"

Romans 8:31
"...If God is for us, who can be against us?"

John 8:11
"And Jesus said, "I do Not condemn you either.
Go, and from now on do not sin anymore."

A Pen sketch taken from John 8:1-11,15

Come, walk with me to the temple in Jerusalem. It's a beautiful morning and who knows, Jesus may be there again, today. I can't wait to hear His words, messages, and stories again! It's so different, so full of power and love. I marvel at all the people He heals with such miraculous power and even forgives and acquits of their sin... I wonder what He's going to do today.

Do you hear the sound of footsteps? Everyone is rushing to the temple. Hey look, Jesus and His disciples are walking down the Mount of Olives! They say He prays alone on the mountain.

Yes, there's the temple. Many people came to worship the Lord. Some are very sincere. Other? Others are coming to "show off". They hope the people will see how holy they live! But I know, the Lord looks deep into our hearts, where only He and I can see... That's where He is looking for our genuine love for Him, our God and Father.

There in the courtyard at the temple, I suddenly heard a whisper, a stirring, an excitement... "It's Jesus!" "He's here too!" People are starting to crowd together, they want to see what He's going to do today, what new message He has for us today...?

But the church leaders, the Pharisees and scribes are angry! Jesus is not welcome here. He just upsets everything with His "new strange" messages and the things He does! No, Jesus gets too much attention!

What's going on there?! It's a big noise and a woman is groaning and shouting: "No, leave me alone! Leave me...!" The woman is forcibly dragged closer and pushed in between the crowd surrounding Jesus. She is roughly pushed, so that she falls wildly to the ground, headfirst at the feet of Jesus.

Her face, now red with shame. Blood flows freely from a wound on her forehead, after the fall. She feels horrible, and she knows she has sinned, she has been caught out, guilty and now doomed to death...!! She knows the punishment and there is no way out, she knows what the law says! In her mind's eye, she sees her entire miserable life playing out in front of her. From an early age, abused, molested, counted a worthless thing in the eyes of her father and brothers, cast out on the street to work out her own life. No one even wanted to allow her to clean their homes, for she herself was considered unclean. What else could she do? A life on the street, full of seduction and just a few pieces of money to take care of tomorrow... That's the only way that she feels kind of "accepted." Now this... The humiliation just never stops!

When she looked up and met Jesus' eyes, the tears of guilt, brokenness, and humiliation caught up with her and drenched her face so that everything became misty...

WHO IS THIS MAN who speaks with such Godly love and compassion, but also has such an authoritative conduct? Why should she be humiliated before Him? Is it not enough that she has already been sentenced to death according to the law? Yes, she must be killed with stones! Everyone points their finger at her. She's bad, a total worthless person! A zero in everyone's eyes! She's not even worth getting so close to the temple and now she is in the temple courtyard!

Have you felt like that in your life before? Perhaps you are feeling like that right now? No one wants to know you or talk to you. According to them, you are totally "useless". When you needed someone to believe in you, not even one person, not even the one you thought was closest to you, who you thought cared about you and who you love most, wanted to know you! No, you're alone, abandoned, unjustly condemned, and now you must take the punishment alone.

This woman often felt, just like you, when she thought she had found a friend, she was abused, let down. He even pointed his finger at her.

The church leaders, the holy saints want to stone her to death! She deserves it, she committed the sin for it. She is by no means an asset to society, no, she is rather a threat that tempts others! "Life would be a better place without her," they say.

BUT...

She is not alone, and neither are you! Jesus is with you and with her. Jesus who shows endless, eternal love, mercy, and forgives sins. He is here with you today and he sees you specifically. He sees deep down inside your heart and knows who and what you really are.

Jesus knew this woman was very precious. He formed her with His own hands, created into a perfect image. He also made you so special, with so much care. Jesus knows and sees her just as she really is. He sees the beauty that He deposited into her, waiting to develop to its fullness, even though life has caused her heart to break into pieces... **That's why He is here to heal her, and not to condemn her. Jesus came to preach, live, and demonstrate a new life through His Gospel. He did not only preach it, but He also lived it as an example to everyone. He did not expect anything that He was not prepared to do. A new dispensation was breaking, but the "high and holy saints" did not recognize or notice it. They were caught up in the "right and wrong" doings of the law and not living a life of Godly love conduct.**

You know, **Jesus is saying to you again today, you are His. He made you special. You are unique and precious. He holds your hand very tightly, and even when you think you've relaxed your grip on Him, He is still holding you. "You are Mine, I know your name," says the Lord, "Look, it is written in the palm of my hand! You are not forgotten!" I am carrying you from your mother's womb and will carry you into your old age." I will never leave you nor forsake you." I am your God." I am the love you are seeking." "Nothing and no one can snatch you out of My hand. I will not release My grip on you."**

Jesus has already chosen this sinful woman for His kingdom, for He sees her potential as a blood-washed child of God. Useful, happy in His eternal Love and a vessel of honor to glorify God the Father.

Jesus **said, "Let him who is without sin cast the first stone..."** No one can tell us what else He wrote in the sand, that day, but it was enough... Without sin? No, no one!

That day a sinner experienced His grace, mercy, forgiveness, and love, when Jesus said to her: "<u>Neither do I condemn you. Go and sin no more</u>." In the midst of her forgiveness, she

64

also experienced Jesus' hand of healing on her broken heart and spirit. She heard the prophet Isaiah's prophetic words echo in her mind: "He sent Me to heal those who are crushed in heart.... to release those who are broken..." and she realized that she is experiencing the fulfillment of it, now in her own life.

Satan accuses you and me day and night at the throne of our Heavenly Father: "This child, man or woman, is bad and worthless. Look at what he or she has done! They do not deserve to be part of the heavenly kingdom! They deserve to die in hell!" Our so-called friends, colleagues, even family often also stand ready to point out our weaknesses and condemn us, but Jesus is also there, **He stands ready to say to God, our Father: "I also died for this one! My blood cleansed him or her from all sin and iniquity. I have prepared their place in our heavenly kingdom. She, he is MINE!"**

Jesus came to fulfill the law on our behalf, knowing that in our sinful state we are incapable of doing so. He even came to take our punishment on Him and redeem us from the sin and death we deserve based on the law. He has forgiven your sins and justified you and come to live out the principles of God's kingdom so that we have His Example to follow. He fulfilled the law and established a new dispensation with His law for us. That's the law of love. He brought a new Gospel, one of freedom in Jesus Christ and one that lays down the principles of God's kingdom for us.

Do you often feel abandoned and alone?
All broken and despondent and worthless?
Just be still and feel the hand of Jesus now
resting on your shoulder.
Jesus is saying to you, "You are not alone.
You are precious in My sight.
I love you with an eternal love.
I called you by your name, you know.
"You are Mine!"

Additional Scriptures to read:

Isaiah 43:1b-4b,5a,13b,18,19,25
John 10:28–29
Isaiah 46:3b–4
Colossian 3:13,12
Hebrews 2:18
1 John 1:7–9

Psalm 145:14
Isaiah 49:15–16
Psalm 147:3
Revelation 12:10b,11
Hebrews 9:11,12,24
Luke 4:17–19

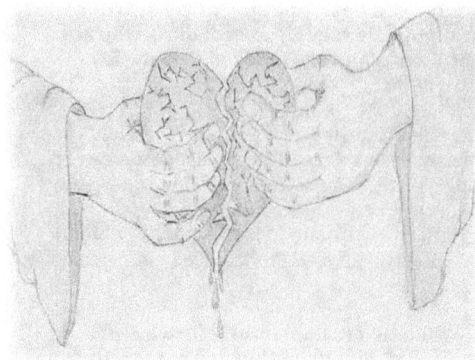

BROKEN HEARTS

A heart...
Shattered, crushed
Into thousand pieces...

A notice erected:
"Heart uninhabitable
Ready for demolition..."

Why is it so broken?
O, the thoughts of pain...
Happy memories
Now all shattered
Left cold, abandoned
Surrounded by high walls
In solitary "protection."

Protection? No!
Not even by a chance!
A heart filled with anger
Hatred, envy & bitterness.

Trampled love...
Suffocated by unforgiveness
No more passion & excitement
All is lost in the painful darkness.

But wait a minute,
Do you see the Light?
Do you feel the warm heartbeat?
Do you feel the New Life?
Breaking through the darkness
Do you hear it?

"A crushed reed
He will not break, ..."
"A dim wick
He will not extinguish..."
He supports you
when you fall
He lifts you up
When you are bent over
of your burden..."
"He heals the broken-hearted
He binds up their wounds"

JESUS is His Name!
Perfect, Infallible,
Wonderful, Eternal Love!
For you and me
Grace, mercy & forgiveness
Given to us,
to share in love
Behold, all things are made new.
Touched by God Himself!

Written by SE De Jager

66

III.   *STEP BY STEP WITH JESUS...*

Colossians 2:6,7
"Therefore, just as you received Christ Jesus as Lord, continue to live your lives in Him, rooted and built up in Him and firm in your faith just as you were taught, and overflowing with thankfulness"

1 Peter 2:21
"For to this you were called, since Christ also suffered for you, leaving an example for you to follow in His steps."

ON THE ROAD OF LIFE

Years come and pass
Full of memories of yesterdays
Long since passed
Some filled with happiness and joy
others filled with heartache & pain
Sometimes Full of Mercy & Love
Sent from our Abba Father from above.

Days, weeks, months,
Lay stretched out
Future still to come...
No fear needs to prevail
For Jesus walks with us
His love, mercy and grace
Is to strengthen us day by day.

In your hand,
The pen of life
To write events & memories
Created for today
All written in your own book of life
Written in your heart.

The choice is yours
What will you write today?
Will it be moments of destruction?
Will it be moments of grief and pain?
What message will you leave
In other hearts today?
OR
Are you sowing love seeds?
In another's heart today?
Moments of shared peace & joy
Reflecting God's eternal light
In dark & needy hearts, today?

We cannot change the past
Yet, the present
Is in our hands
To create God-given memories
If we should choose to do so.

Forget what's behind
Stretch out to what's ahead
Chase Your High Calling
in Christ Jesus...
Have faith in Him.
So that you may finish the race
And enter into eternity with Jesus
Your Savior and King.

Written by Sharon E De Jager

AT THE FEET OF JESUS

*"Now as they went on their way, Jesus entered a certain village
where a woman named Martha welcomed Him as a guest.
She had a sister named Mary, who sat at the Lord's feet and
listened to what He said.
But Martha was distracted with all the preparations she had to make,
so, she came up to Him and said, "Lord, don't you care
that my sister has left me to do all the work alone?
Tell her to help me." But the Lord answered her,
"Martha, Martha, you are worried and troubled about many things,
but one thing is needed. Mary has chosen the best part,
it will not be taken away from her."*
Luke 10:38-42

Busy, busy, always busy. No time to stop and reflect on what and who keeps me occupied! We get caught up in the mill of life and when we are finally brought to a standstill because of some kind of crisis, we realize how "empty" we have actually become. It is an emptiness that has drained our inner powers and leaves us no reserve to fall back on in times of crisis. It forces us to pause for a moment and reflect on these two questions: -

- **Does that which we are busy with, have eternal value or not?**
- **When was the last time that you sat peacefully at the feet of Jesus, enjoying some quality time with Him?**

One of Satan's greatest attack techniques is to make our lives so busy that we have no time for God. Sometimes we get so busy with the things of the Lord and don't make time to be busy with the Lord Himself who is the Source of power and strength, provided to us, to do His things!

Remember, it's like a kettle that can only boil the water when it is plugged into the wall plug and turned on. Without the power source, the kettle is powerless and not in the ability to warm up and boil the water.

Who or what is your source of strength in life?

<u>What are the consequences of a hectic way of life in which there is no time to sit at the feet of</u> Jesus?
  - ➢ We don't only stagnate spiritually, we're moving backwards into our old way of living, separate from God. There is no "standing still" in spiritual life. You're moving either forwards or backwards. **A spiritual decline leads to spiritual death!**

  - ➢ The world and all our life obligations drain us emotionally, mentally, and even physically. There is rarely a moment when life out there, ploughs something back into our lives. If you and I are spiritually empty, we are also **drained of the spiritual strength and abilities** we should have in the Lord.

In Matthew 13:15, Jesus says: "**For the heart of this people has become dull; they are hard of hearing, and they have shut their eyes, that they would not see with their eyes and hear with their ears and understand with their hearts and turn, and I would heal them.**"
Jesus describes in Matthew 13:15 three aspects of man's spiritual condition, when there is no time spent with Him: -

➢ Your **heart becomes "dull."** In other words, you lose your sensitivity to God's presence in your life. It's a serious condition that causes you to no longer live in dependence on the Lord. You start living in the deceitfulness of the world around you, allowing it to form your perceptions on life, not allowing Jesus to do so, through His Spirit.

➢ **Spiritual deafness** to the voice of the Holy Spirit. Jesus says that we "hardly" hear what He says. We're going to look for answers from other people, only to end up being deceived. Jeremiah 17:5-6 points out that you will be like a bare tree in the wilderness and dry places, but if you trust in the Lord, it will be different.

➢ **Spiritual blindness** also follows, for Jesus says that the people close their eyes. We lose our awareness of God's hand in a matter, because in principle our life is darkened. Jeremiah 17:6 makes it clear that the man who does not rely on the Lord will not see when good comes. In other words, he will not be able to see the good that God works for him because he has lost his sensitivity to God. The problem is that one soon chooses not to see God's hand and influence in our lives because the activities of the world are becoming more important to us. This makes our lives darkened, because the Light of Jesus no longer shines in it as described in Matthew 6:22,23.

➢ The end of a way of life in which we have systematically moved the Lord out is the **decay of our roots in life.** We no longer walk in Jesus with our roots in Him. We are rooted in other areas of life. Colossians 2:6-7 **exhorts us to walk in Jesus, rooted and built up in Him**. Soon we begin to make decisions according to our own insights and no longer according to the insight God gives us through His Holy Spirit. This results in us often making wrong choices that can have further negative consequences. Proverbs 16:25 says that we think we are on the right track, only to find out that it leads to death.

➢ Another consequence is that we no longer have an awareness in us regarding the power God can work in our lives to deal with problems. When the crisis comes, we happen to remember Him and then want to appeal to His help and power. If he doesn't help us, we are rebellious. The problem is that our own sins have **formed a barrier between us and God.** See Isaiah 59:1,2.

➢ We become **ignorant in God's Word** and ignorance makes us often act outside of God's will. What should not be forgotten is that Satan is well aware of God's principles and just waiting for us to move outside that framework so that we can be attacked by him. That's when he accuses us in the Lord's presence, looking for a good reason to cause us harm.

➢ The **spiritual doors open** and the destroyer, Satan, steps in.... read John 10:10 & John 8:44.

➢ These negative consequences sour through to our marriage, family and interpersonal relationships and can give rise to **broken hearts and lives.**

In short, we are in trouble!

In Matthew 6:33 and Psalm 37:4, we are exhorted to seek first the kingdom of God and to delight in the Lord before we can expect any prosperity at all. Unfortunately, we often only look at our circumstances and lose perspective on what is truly important. The appointment with the Lord is postponed and in due course not upheld.

In In Matthew 11:28-30, Jesus invites us with these words: "Come to Me, all you who are weary and burdened, and I will give you rest. Take My yoke on you and learn from Me, because I am gentle and humble in heart, and you will find rest for your souls. For My yoke is easy to bear, and My load is not hard to carry. With Him we will find rest for spirit, soul, and body.

The choice is for you and me to make... Are we going to allow the anxieties and obligations of life to keep us so busy that we make no time for God at all? Are we willing to live with the above consequences and eventually forfeit everlasting life?

<u>What are the consequences of a regular quality appointment at the feet of Jesus?</u>

❖ You and I will be **planted like a tree by streams of water**, we will bear fruit, regardless of the seasons and our leaves will not wither. It is described in Psalm 1:3 & Jeremiah 17:7,8.
Have you ever wondered what the symbolism behind this description is?
The tree is you and me.
The streams of water are symbolic of the Life-Giving Word of God, revealed by His Spirit in our hearts. As I mentioned earlier, we are recommended to keep our lives rooted in Jesus. And the fruit? It is the manifestation of the presence of the Holy Spirit in you. Please read Galatians 5:22 about this. Notice that the Bible says that the leaves of your tree of life will not wither. When we are rooted in Jesus and regularly put ourselves at the feet of Jesus so that we can become spiritually full, we will be able to deal with the crises of life in His power, without becoming discouraged.

❖ In Matthew 25:3-12,13, Jesus tells the story of the 10 virgins waiting to attend the wedding feast. Five of them were ready for the unforeseen and five did not provide for the unforeseen occurrences. As their lamps needed oil to take them through the night, so we need the oil of the Holy Spirit to sustain us through hard times. Having this **Holy Spirit oil** requires that we make time to sit at the feet of Jesus so that we can continually build an intimate relationship with Him that will ensure that the Holy Spirit actively works in our lives.

❖ Within the framework of God's principles and an active, intimate growing relationship with Him, you and I also enjoy **God's** protection. Zechariah 2:5 tells us that God will be a fiery wall around us (just as He promised to Israel) We read in Psalm 34:8: "**The LORD's angel camps around the LORD's loyal followers and delivers them. Taste and see that the LORD is good! How blessed is the one who takes shelter in Him! Remain loyal to the LORD, you chosen people of His, for His loyal followers lack nothing!** "

❖ The miracle of regular encounters with Jesus is that our **relationship with Him** is **growing.** There will be no spiritual decline because the Lord makes us so full of His presence and power that we will experience that "living waters flow from within us", as Jesus says in John 7:37-39. We will be spiritually satisfied to overflowing, thereby knowing the joy of the Lord. David also writes of this in Psalm 23 when he says: "Thou anoint my head with oil; my cup runs over..."

❖ Jesus **promises** to write His Principles and **Word on the tablets of our heart and engrave it in our minds** so that we will not be ignorant of His will. Hebrews 10:15-17.

❖ We will enjoy the **enduring presence of Jesus through His Spirit** that will comfort, guide, help and teach us. Read John 16:13 & John 14:17,26 please. The Holy Spirit will enlighten **our spiritual eyes and our spiritual ears will get used to His voice, once again.** See Ephesians 1:17,18.

❖ God becomes a refuge for us in times of need, a Rock that gives steadfastness. Read Proverbs 18:10. When we rely on the Lord while making our plans, all things will work out for good, because we **live in dependence on Him.** Proverbs 19:21 & Proverbs 16:9 says more about this fact. Our lives will not be powerless, because we rely not on our own strength, but on God's.

❖ During this time with the Lord, we will find that **He reveals Himself to us and will reveal His secrets to us.** Jesus promised that it would be so in John 14:21,23. Moreover, He will take up residence with us. It testifies to an intimate relationship of trust between you and the Lord, one in which He is willing to share His precious secrets with you. Psalm 25:14 describes this fact very well when David writes: "The secret of the LORD is with them that fear Him; and He will shew (establish/show) them His covenant."

These are just a few of the abundant blessings we will enjoy.

Paul also spoke of this constant struggle between spirit and flesh in Galatians 5:16-21 and in Romans 7:23,26. The flesh is constantly calling to be satisfied by temporary worldly things while the Spirit urges us to be occupied with what is in line with God's will. In Romans 7:22, Paul explains the struggle between Spirit and flesh and that he makes a conscious choice to revel in the "law of God, which is the law of the Spirit and Love, after the inner man." The delight in the Lord's Word brings about a positive change in our mind and thinking that will progressively dominate the needs of the flesh. In James 1:21b, James explains how the **implanted Word** has the power to save our souls. So, we must not only be hearers of the Word of the Lord but become doers. In this way, we will develop deeper insight into the "perfect law of freedom" in Jesus Christ. Read about this in James 1:22–25.

It is time that we do not allow the demands of this earthly life keep us away from a quality encounter with God. Let us become like Mary, who chose to sit at Jesus' feet and listen to Him and His teaching, rather than being very busy and concerned with the temporal things of this world like Martha. Mary had her priorities right in line with God's will.

Jesus answers Martha in Luke 10:41-42: "**But the Lord answered her, "Martha, Martha, you are worried and troubled about many things, but one thing is needed. Mary has chosen the best part; it will not be taken away from her."**

Abba Father forgive us for neglecting our time with You,
help us to choose to be occupied with those things
that have eternal value and
will establish your Kingdom on earth.
In Jesus' Name Alone
Amen.

BE WATCHFUL NOT TO DEPART FROM YOUR FIRST LOVE

"But I have this against you: You have departed from your first love!"
Revelation 2:4

A man or a woman who is convinced that they have discovered the true love of their life will do anything blindly to convey this message of love to their partner. Such a person eats, drinks, sleeps, and lives for that special love in their life. The first thought with which they wake up and the last thought with which they fall asleep revolves around this one person they love so much. Everything planned is planned with this love in mind. The more time they can spend in each other's company, the better. Suddenly, his or her own needs don't matter so much anymore. The greatest wish of the heart is to see that special person happy. Soon they begin to dream together of a life in which they can be together forever. The fire of love burns high in their hearts.

With the utmost sincerity, the bride and the bridegroom lay down the marriage promise. There is no thought of any negativity or hardship, just happiness, prosperity, and fulfillment. Yet the rosiness of this love decreases over a period of time and then love is tested by the demands of life. The demands of life stretch and stretch this love in all directions, sometimes to a thin thread that can easily break and shoot back, with only the remnants remaining scattered, lying in a relentless society that do not care.

WHAT DOES THE LOVE OF OUR LIVES LOOK LIKE? WILL IT BE ABLE TO WITHSTAND THE TEST? WILL IT STAND FIRM OR NOT?

God looks at us as human beings and loves us with an eternal, perfect, steadfast love. His love burns high but does not consume the one on whom He pours it out. It is symbolically defined in the Song of Solomon 8:6b and verse 7b. His love raises us up from our precarious sinful state, heals our spirit and soul, and creates a new joy within us that will continue even during difficult circumstances. Isaiah 61:1-3 foretells this for the time when Jesus would arrive as the Messiah. His love brings peace in times of turbulence and carries us through until we can stand again on the summit of victory. His love stood the worst test of all time — death. Even death could not destroy His love for us as confirmed in 1 Corinthians 15:56-58.

He extends His mighty hand to draw us closer so that He can nurture and embrace us in His love that will remain forever. We see in Hosea 11:4 how the Lord reveals His loving character when He calls Ephraim, a tribe of Israel, with love to draw near. God breaks their state of bondage and oppression and takes care of them. The Lord has an unwavering love with which He wants to draw us closer, but it is our choice to accept it or not. He desires to be close to us all the time and pours out many blessings upon us to declare His love for us. In 2 Corinthians 6:16-19, this fact is defined as follows:
"...And what mutual agreement does the temple of God have with idols? **For we are the temple of the living God, just as God said, "I will live in them and will walk among them, and I will be their God, and they will be My people.** Therefore **"come out from their midst, and be separate,"** says the Lord, **"and touch no unclean thing, and I will welcome you, and I will be a Father to you, and you will be My sons and daughters,"** says the All-Powerful Lord."**
God is willing to give us everything necessary to make us taste true, everlasting happiness, but it requires that we also surrender our all to Him.

We see the symbolism throughout the Word of God, how our love relationship with Him is compared to marriage. In the New Testament, the church is compared to the woman in marriage. Paul wrote to the Corinthians in 2 Corinthians 11:2: **"For I am jealous for you with** godly jealousy, because <u>I promised you in marriage to one husband, to present you as a pure virgin to Christ.</u>" In Revelation we see how Jesus is the Bridegroom of all time preparing to meet His bride, namely us, the true "Ecclesia" church, so that we may be with Him forever. He wants to clothe us with a white bridal robe of righteousness and make us sit at a banquet to celebrate our unification with Him. Please read Revelation 19:7,8 about this future happening.

He has long since made His love covenant with us and is now waiting for us to make the final choice to accept His love with surrender.

Some of us refuse this love offer, others accept it wholeheartedly and work with all their heart to strengthen their love relationship with the King of all kings. There is another group that does accept this love offer from the Lord and initially diligently work on their love relationship with Him, but systematically the zeal and rosiness decrease, as the trials of life come to stretch this love relationship between them and God. It is stretched to the limit.

Jesus had a serious message to the congregation of Ephesus: "I know your works and your labor and your endurance.... **But I have this against you that you have departed from your first love**. ... <u>**Repent and do the first works....**</u>" Revelation 2:2-5.
Here were a few people who experienced God's love, but who soon began to turn away from the love that was once so wonderful to them. They were initially zealous in their love for the Lord and joyfully did the will of God. They loved Him with a similar love as between a bride and the bridegroom. What made them turn away from their First Love, which was Jesus??

So often it happens that marriages are destroyed by the faintest excuses. People so easily turn away from the love that once filled their entire life abundantly. Suddenly, it's not there anymore... Why not? What went wrong? Why turn away from this exciting first love?

When we are in a love relationship with Jesus, it is far deeper than any love we can experience in a human relationship. Just as Jesus is fully dedicated to always demonstrating His love toward us, He is waiting for us to do the same. This love cannot only be built on emotions. It needs a much deeper foundation which only God can instill within our hearts. It is also a love by choice which we are determined to maintain, irrespective of circumstances.

In Genesis 22:2,9-18, God gave Abraham the most difficult choice imaginable. He told Abraham to sacrifice his only covenant-son to Him according to the regulations He had laid down. This was a great test for Abraham, for Isaac was the child in which the divine promise of his offspring was incarcerated. How could God ask that of him? **Abraham's love and faith in the Lord were far greater than this promise and his own desires. He trusted God fully as the One who works all things together for good, regardless of the circumstances in which he currently finds himself. Abraham loved God with an unwavering love.** In Hebrews 11:17-18, we see that Abraham believed that God would raise his son from the dead. So, he tackles this difficult task in obedience, unaware of what God will do for him. **Abraham's love for the Lord is stretched, and tested to the limit,** but God wanted to see the "ultimate" of Abraham's Love for Him, demonstrated. "Do not harm the boy!" the angel said. "Do not do anything to him, for now I know that you fear God because you did not withhold your son, your only son, from Me." As said in Genesis 22:12.
God provides a ram for the burnt offering, and Isaac becomes the beginning of Abraham's seed.

TO WHAT EXTREME CAN YOUR LOVE FOR THE LORD BE EXTENDED? IS JESUS REALLY YOUR FIRST LOVE? ARE YOU AND HE IN A LOVE RELATIONSHIP, LIKE THAT OF A YOUNG BRIDE AND GROOM?
In Deuteronomy 10:12, and Micah 6:8 God explains to us what He desires of us. In summary:
- **That you will fear the Lord**
- **That you will walk in all His ways**

- **That you will love Him.**
- **That you will serve Him...**
   ... With all your heart and with all your soul...

Perhaps you think it was only for the Old Testament dispensation, but Jesus Himself comes into the New Testament dispensation and repeats this desire in Mark 12:29-33, with the following words:

"Jesus answered, "The most important is: '**Listen, Israel, the Lord our God, the Lord is One. Love the Lord your God with all your heart, with all your soul, with all your mind, and with all your strength.'** The second is: '**Love your neighbor as yourself.'** There is no other commandment greater than these.

The expert in the law said to him, "That is true, Teacher; you are right to say that He is one, and there is no one else besides Him. And to love Him with all your heart, with all your mind, and with all your strength and to love your neighbor as yourself is more important than all burnt offerings and sacrifices."

Our love for Jesus is demonstrated in our daily walk with Him. To keep the Love fire between God and ourselves burning, requires a changed and disciplined way of life. This love requires quality time with Jesus, in His presence, so that we can get to know His will, serve, and obey Him with joy. It requires a sensitivity to God's desires for our lives by setting our spiritual ears and eyes on His voice. He promises in His Word, the Bible, that through His Spirit He will teach and guide us in heavenly truth and make known to us the things to come, that He will be our Comforter and Helper. Read about this in John 14:16,17,26,27 & John 16:13.

This love is self-sacrificing, unselfish, always ready to serve, always ready to put a smile on Jesus' face by demonstrating His love to our neighbor, in all sincerity, not seeking our own glory, but rather honoring Jesus.

It is necessary to lose yourself in full surrender in God's love so that He can purify, mold, and make you a vessel of honor for His glory, useful in His loving hands. See 2 Timothy 2:21. We always have the assurance that when God is at work in our lives, it is not devastating, but upbuilding. Read Isaiah 42:3.

Sometimes we need to self-examine and give the Holy Spirit a chance to search our hearts for those people or things that have replaced our first love for Jesus. In Romans 8:26,27 we read of how the Holy Spirit searches our hearts. When we become aware of what replaced our first love for Jesus, it is time to offer a love offering to God, like Abraham. That which has come between us and God is laid down on the altar. It is not a pleasant practice, but necessary to keep our lives in the right relationship with God. Amid this serious choice, we can expect to enter into a deeper dimension in our love relationship with God.

When we seek His face in prayer and sincerely confess that we have left our first love but want to return to Him, we lay down, that other love on the altar before Him, and we will experience once again as God purifies our hearts and once again drench us with His eternal love. You will be a changed person — a new person in Christ. You will find yourself in a deeper dimension of God's love.

Jesus looks deep into our hearts, where the truth about ourselves lies. He knows the price of our choice of our love offering to Him. Therefore, this sacrifice will not pass Him by, unnoticed.

As the bridegroom desires to wrap his bride in his arms of love, care and promises of blessing and prosperity, so Jesus wants to wrap you up too. Return to His loving arms and drink from the cup of His eternal, perfect love. There is no better place to be than in the center of Jesus' love!!

"Love Jesus deeply and sincerely.
Let your love be known to all people.
As He loves you, so must your love be.
Let your love be powerful and undefeated.
Let your love be passionate and purposeful.
No matter who or what resists,
Don't weaken!
Stand firm against the darkness of this age!
And let your love flow from your innermost being!
Let your love be with surrender,
A love from your Heart, Spirit, Mind & Soul...
This is the path back to God's heart.
The true way to eternal life.
It is the path that leads to true, lasting,
abundant Happiness!
That happiness that can be found
only in Jesus Christ."

MIRRORS...

1 Corinthians 13:12
"For now, we see in a mirror indirectly, but then we will see face to face.
Now I know in part, but then I will know fully,
just as I have been fully known."

2 Corinthians 3:18
"And we all, with unveiled faces reflecting the glory of the Lord,
are being transformed into the same image from one degree of glory to another,
which is from the Lord, who is the Spirit."

We too often look in the mirror of the past and then see ourselves within the framework of our mistakes, blunders, failures, and weaknesses of the past. It distorts our own true image in the mirror. Yet God asks us not to look through the glasses of our own weaknesses, failures, and mistakes, but rather to look ahead. In Paul's words..." from face to face..." Because it's looking ahead, not backwards.

1 Corinthians 13 is the famous chapter in which divine love is defined in practice. It's as if Paul is looking at himself as he looks at Jesus in the mirror. Jesus is the all-encompassing realization of true love, so he can measure himself against this "mirror" of love. 1 John 4:16 tells us this too.

Jesus, in Matthew 22:37-39 and Mark 12:29-31, reaffirmed the commandment of love at the end of the second commandment, saying that you must love your neighbor **as yourself.** In other words, **if you have no healthy balanced self-love, you are incapable of loving others.**

In Isaiah 43:18, God says: "Do not consider the former things, nor consider the things of old. Behold, I will do a new thing; now it shall spring forth; will ye not know it? I make a way in the wilderness, rivers in the wilderness." Here the Lord gives a wonderful promise. It is the promise of Jesus that would come to change the circumstances of that time. Jesus would make a way in the wilderness, for He is the Way of Truth and Life. Jesus would bring rivers into the wilderness... Water is indicative of the life-giving Word of the Lord. Jesus brought a new fresh Gospel of the Kingdom of Heaven in which He came to disclose the detail of the kingdom principles and His Gospel of new life. It is this new life-giving river that has brought new life into the barren land of the wilderness, which is in fact, our hearts' condition. If we kept reflecting on the past's events where the law spelled out our punishment and made our sins clear, we would never have been able to recognize Jesus as our Savior and Eternal Father. We could not seize His love, grace, forgiveness, and mercy and share His healing of spirit, soul, and body. The experts of the law, Pharisees, and Sadducees, as well as the common people were so caught up in the law that they could not claim Jesus as their Savior and King, their long-awaited Messiah.

In Luke 9:62 "Jesus said to him, "No one who puts his hand to the plow and looks back is fit for the kingdom of God."
At that time, the habit existed to gather a dead person's dead bones after a year and then finally lay him/her to rest in the grave prepared for the person. The passing of that person and the lament around it are long gone and **Jesus wants to put the focus of the people on true life, certainly not on death. True life is to be found only in Jesus Christ and His doctrine of God's Kingdom.**

It is these new things of God that only become ours when we look at ourselves in the mirror with a new vision, leaving the past in His hands. As the latter man was admonished not to look backwards, we are also admonished to put our focus on Jesus and let go of the past.

IT'S TIME TO GIVE THIS MIRROR TO JESUS AND THEN, TO TURN TO THE MIRROR OF THE CROSS.

What we see through our own eyes in the mirror of life is often a "borrowed" image shaped by the world and community in which we move and live. Yet the Lord looks at us with different eyes, so Paul could write under inspiration from the Holy Spirit: **"But God has chosen the foolish things of the world to shame the wise. And God has chosen the weak things of the world to put to shame the things that are strong. And God hath chosen that which is dishonorable in the world, and that which is despised, and that which is not, to set aside what is regarded as something.** " As written in 1 Corinthians 1:27,28. WOW! It's the best picture of myself I'd ever want to see in the mirror! God considers me worth more than all the world's wisdom, noble, and strong! He makes my useless "0" a "100%+" in this world! What more could I ask for? What God thinks of me and the value He attaches to my life, is far more precious than that of the world around me! Moreover, He called me to follow through on His plan.

WHY DID PAUL SAY IN 1 CORINTHIANS 13:12-13 THAT HE SEES IN A MIRROR INDIRECTLY BUT WOULD ONE DAY SEE FACE TO FACE; NOW HE KNOWS IN PART, BUT ONE DAY HE'LL KNOW FULLY? WHY IS IT LOVE THAT WILL LAST FOREVER?
"For now, we see in a mirror indirectly, but then we will see face to face. "
We still don't see the full "picture" of God's love, but when Jesus returns or we meet with Him after our death, we will see Him face to face and gain full insight.
"...Now I know in part, but then I will know fully
When we see Jesus face to face, we will gain the full insight we yearn for, insight into love, and many other spiritual concepts.
Why is it love that will last forever?
GOD IS LOVE! That is why love will last forever. Our faith and hope will be fulfilled in that we are in God's heavenly presence and therefore no longer need to hope. Our faith has become a reality.

When we look at ourselves in the mirror of the cross, we see Jesus saying to us: "You are precious to Me, so precious that I have sacrificed My life for you on the cross, that you may live forever. I don't look at your mistakes and failures, it's already wiped out with My blood. Read 1 John 1:7. You can live in the freedom of My forgiveness and grace as defined in John 8:32,36. I see the man I created from the beginning. This man who was created with Divine potential, to live in victory, to live intimately with Me... You, My Child, you must choose to fulfill and realize My potential in you. You must choose to detach yourself from the past and look at yourself through My eyes. I know what I have planned about you — a Joyous Life of Prosperity and Love, not of evil and adversity. Now choose not to look back and die in yourself but choose the life I give you."

It's time to put on God's glasses and look back in the mirror and see ourselves as God sees us. That's the perspective of his love.

Look at yourself from your position in Jesus Christ and see the image with which Abba Father created you.

Abba Father, help me to see myself as You see me.
I surrender my past, weaknesses, failures, mistakes
into Your hands
Thank You for washing my life white as snow
in the blood of Jesus Christ.
Thank You for giving me a new vision and
letting me find my self-worth in You.
I praise Your Name and bring You honor.
In Jesus' Name alone.
Amen.

BUILDING BLOCKS FOR AN EXCELLENT FAITH

2 Peter 1:1-8

1 Peter 1:5-8

"For this very reason, make every effort to <u>add to your faith excellence</u>, to excellence, <u>knowledge</u>; to knowledge, <u>self-control</u>; to self-control, <u>perseverance</u>; to perseverance, <u>godliness</u>; to godliness, <u>brotherly affection</u>; to brotherly affection, <u>unselfish love</u>. For if these things are really yours and are <u>continually increasing, they will keep you from becoming ineffective and unproductive in your pursuit of knowing our Lord Jesus Christ more intimately.</u>

WHAT IS FAITH?

To understand why the above-mentioned building blocks are needed for an excellent faith, we first need to know what faith really is and what it consists of.

Hebrews 11:1 defines faith as follows: -

*" Now faith is the substance of things hoped for,
*The evidence of things not seen."

In Romans 4:17-21 we read about Abraham's unwavering faith and how God calls that which does not yet exist, into existence as if it already existed beforehand: "... (as it is written, "**I have made you the father of many nations**"). He is our father in the presence of God whom he believed – **the God who makes the dead alive and summons the things that do not yet exist as though they already do.** Against all hope Abraham believed in God as his only hope, with the result that he became **the father of many nations** according to the pronouncement, "**so will your descendants be.**" Without being weak in faith, he considered his own body as dead (because he was about one hundred years old) and the deadness of Sarah's womb. **He did not waver in unbelief about the promise of God but was strengthened in faith, giving glory to God. He was fully convinced that what God promised he was also able to do**. So indeed, **it was credited to Abraham as righteousness.**

Abraham **believed against all negative circumstances and was fully convinced that God will do** what He had promised, and he finally received it. He waited 25 years for the fulfillment of the promise. "Now faith is being sure of what we hope for, being convinced of what we do not see." (NET)

What are the characteristics of faith?
What faith is NOT:

➤ Faith is **not** some mystical exercise or "power" with which we twist God's arm to give us or do what we ask for.
➤ Faith is also not a command with which we enforce the Lord's "services".
➤ Faith is not a means by which we claim that the Lord does certain things for us.
➤ Faith is not a product of reasoning of our fleshly mind, but a product of our born-again spirit.

Faith IS....

❖ Faith is generated from the Truthful Word of God in the Bible. Romans 10:17 says, "So then faith comes by hearing, and hearing by the word of God." In other words, faith is generated by hearing the Word of the Lord.
❖ Faith produces results when it is in line with God's Word, we have a hope, expectation, and firm trust in God's all-powerful abilities.
❖ Faith is also to see, **with our spiritual eyes,** the thing we believe will happen, and then act as if it had already happened.

❖ **Faith generates an expectation and hope that becomes the driving force of our faith. Furthermore, faith is <u>not</u> rooted in our own abilities, but in the surpassing ability of God.**

The moment that, that which we believed will happen, happened, it is no longer faith, but a concrete fact and reality, a manifestation, as well as proof of our faith.

<u>**To maintain and strengthen our faith, we need spiritual building blocks.**</u>
Peter encourages us to work diligently to cultivate an **excellent faith.**
We need to add the following spiritual qualities to our faith: -
- Excellence
- Knowledge
- Self-control
- Perseverance
- Godliness
- Brotherly affection
- Unselfish Love

Excellence
Excellence is indicative of the quality of faith we build on. The Greek according to G703, is "arete" which carries the following meaning "excellence" or "valor," which confirms the translation used in this verse. So, we should strive to build an outstanding excellent faith.

Knowledge
Without **knowledge,** faith cannot be born. Knowledge of what or who?
In Hosea 4:6,7, the Lord explains that without spiritual knowledge of God and His will and Kingdom principles, we, like Israel, immerse ourselves in sin, because we violate His principles, which we do not know. Thereby, we are becoming an open target for Satan who diligently attacks and harasses us. The problem is that we often make a conscious choice not to spend time with God and His Word, and as a result, our relationship with Him and our faith does not grow!

Romans 10:17 explains that our faith is built through hearing the Word of God which increases our spiritual knowledge and insight into God's will.
2 Peter 1:1 - 3, points out that knowing Jesus' blessed power that works in us resulting in us obtaining righteousness before God, when we allow it, becomes the foundation of our faith in God.

We need to have knowledge of God's character and His principles so that our faith can be healthy and in the right perspective. In other words, what we believe must be in line with God's will and character. If we then ask God for something in faith, we will receive it, because we will know to ask and believe in line with His will. Jesus Himself says that if we believe, anything is possible. See also Mark 9:23.

In Hosea 6:2,3,6, the Lord tells us that we must pursue knowledge of Him, make an effort to know Him, for through it a love relationship with Him will develop and the result is that He will breathe new life into our lives and that the rains of His abundant blessing will come down on our lives. The deeper we dig into the Word of God, the stronger and more steadfast our relationship with Him becomes, the more the working of His Spirit becomes in us and the stronger our love and faith in Him becomes.
Knowledge of God and His Word also makes us mentally resistant so that we can resist Satan. The Holy Spirit makes the Word alive within us and the influence of the **Word,** when we

confess it, is validated by the Holy Spirit to such an extent that Satan departs. Read about it in Matthew 4:1-11 & Ephesians 6:17.

We often see that when people come to Jesus with a request, Jesus asks a question that causes the person to **confess** his **faith aloud with his** mouth. We see this in Matthew 9:28. Mark 9:24 In other cases, it was the **people's actions that proved their faith in Jesus as seen in** Matthew 9:2,20-22.

The following **building blocks of faith** become the acts of faith that spur us toward excellent **faith: -**
James 2:17-23,26 points out that faith without works is dead. Faith and actions take hands. Your actions become the proof of what you believe. Therefore, your faith can bring glory to God even before you have received from God the fulfillment of your faith.

Self - Control
Circumstances can often drive us to unreasonable actions, wrong decisions, especially when we are emotionally involved in a case. Temptations can be so appealing that they draw us back to our old sinful life where Jesus had no place. Satan can work through men and woman to test our patience to the limit, and without the help of the Holy Spirit, we can turn to evil and anger that result in sin. Without the guidance of the Holy Spirit, it can also happen that we misapply spiritual knowledge and end up doing more harm than good. (e.g. We can attack someone judgmentally with the Word of God rather than reprove him in love, just because we have not applied self - control with the knowledge we have acquired. Knowledge without Godly wisdom, is dangerous and leads to destruction of especially relationships between people.)

We see in Galatians 5:22 that self-control is one of the fruits of the Holy Spirit.
In 2 Timothy 1:7 we see that the Holy Spirit has not given us a spirit of fear, but of love, power, and self-control.
When we break up the word "self-control," we can say that it means "to control yourself." The best thing is to allow the Holy Spirit to take over that control in your life. It demands a choice on your part to deliberately ask God to take control. When the Holy Spirit is in control, it also takes the impact of our negative emotions out of the situation. Self-control also helps to dispel fear — fear that God won't do what you asked Him to do in faith. Holy Spirit-inspired self-control encourages us to continue to believe in God's surpassing ability against all negative circumstances.

Self-control is also a product of wisdom. It is to know when to keep quiet and when to speak, when to act, and when to leave everything to the Holy Spirit.
2 Timothy 2:15,16,22-25 exhorts us exactly how to exercise self-control in difficult situations and what we should do with temptations. Every situation requires a choice to allow the Holy Spirit to effectively apply self-control from within us, in our situation or not.

Perseverance
Perseverance can also be **connected to persistence and endurance** James 1:2,3 creates the contrast between trial, endurance, and joy. He says that you should view it as a joy when you face hard times, whether through trial or temptation. It can only be a joy when you have **your focus right.** The focus **should be on God,** knowing that God allows the trials to strengthen you spiritually and give you spiritual victories. He empowers you with the ability to endure to the end. Read Philippians 4:13-14. It is the Holy Spirit who works perseverance and determination in you — if you allow Him and don't sit down on Job's proverbial ash heap in discouragement. A negative spirit works a spirit of murmuring and self-pity, which in the end results in failure. **A grateful spirit personally builds us up and generates the perseverance** needed to endure. Read Colossians 3:17 - Philippians 4:6. The positive end result should be in our field of view. It becomes the driving force to push through in God's power. Hebrews 12:2 confirms this

statement. **Jesus is the Perfecter of our faith** and set the very example for us when He endured the cross for our sakes, because He knew that the end result of His suffering, which was victory over death and Satan, a key for every man to gain eternal life and the honored position of sitting at the right hand of God.

Godliness

The Greek word in G2150 and G2152 shed more light on it. The Greek word "eusobeia" means "godliness" and "holiness."
Our **endeavor should be to develop and practice the character qualities of God in our own lives.** We can't get it out of our own strength. It is the working of the Holy Spirit in us that produces it. When we are born again and have the Holy Spirit dwelling within us, it is He who speaks to us to eradicate wrong things in our lives and develop the new qualities of Jesus within us. See Ephesians 4:22,23 & Colossians 3:10.

2 Timothy 2:21 mentions a very important aspect of purification under the hand of God - that we become vessels to the Glory of God, useful in His hands.

In Romans 13:14, we are admonished to clothe ourselves with Jesus Christ, in other words to live out the qualities of Jesus. These qualities are summed up in the fruit of the Holy Spirit in Galatians 5:22. Qualities of the divine nature that are very prominent are God's ability to love; His ability to show mercy and forgive unconditionally.

One thing we must remember, **with the Holy Spirit in us, God's nature is implanted in us. It's our choice whether we're going to let those qualities manifest or not.**

Godliness also involves holiness as defined in the beginning of the section. **Holiness indicates being set apart, set aside for something or someone. In this case, you are set apart for Jesus to do His will and serve Him.**

Brotherly Affection

Notice that there is a distinction between brotherly affection and neighborly love. Brotherly love/affection falls into the category of **love toward our spiritual brothers and sisters in the Lord.** So, besides our love for the Lord, we have a love obligation to the inner circle in which we live.
The Greek word here, is found in G5360 which is the word "philadelphia" and is spoken of as "brotherly kindness."

This is often where we are most tested concerning love in this inner circle. In your close relationship with people, you are necessarily confronted more with their nuances and whims than with the people outside the inner circle. Colossians 3:12-15 gives us clear guidelines regarding love. The most important piece of advice is: "Therefore, as the elect of God, holy and dearly loved, **clothe yourselves with a heart of mercy, kindness, humility, gentleness, and patience bearing with one another and forgiving one another,** if someone happens to have a complaint against anyone else. **Just as the Lord has forgiven you, so you also forgive others. And to all these virtues add love, which is the perfect bond** " This love is possible only when we allow the Holy Spirit to work it out in us. **Romans 5:5 tells us that it is the Holy Spirit who pours out God's love into our hearts.**
Remember, love dies when it is not distributed. The more love we give to others, the more love God will pour out into our hearts.

Neighborly Love

Neighborly love in the context Peter discusses here is expressed in the original Greek in G26 as "agapè" which has the following meaning "affection or benevolence (an act of kindness, a generous gift), charity of love feast." This is the description of divine love and goodwill.
In John 13:34,35, **Jesus says that His love in us will be the mark that we belong to Him.** Do you want to be identified with Jesus? Live God's love in a loveless world!
In 1 John 3:17,18, John exhorts us not only to love with words, but with our deeds!

An active love toward our fellow man is spelled out in Luke 10:30-37 and James 2:16 & Isaiah 58:7,8,10.

Peter's formula for excellent faith is:

> Excellence + Godly Knowledge + Self-control + Perseverance + Godliness + Brotherly Affection + Neighborly Love = Excellent Quality Faith

Quality faith is indispensable in our fight against Satan. 2 Peter 1:8,9 warns us that if it is not present within us, we are spiritually **blind,** and visionless. Moreover, we are in danger of falling back into our old sinful way of life and forgetting the righteousness we have obtained in Christ.

Quality, excellent faith requires an active, growing, love relationship with God.
Quality belief with all the above qualities summarized in it must always be in motion. It must grow constantly and not become static. (v. 8). **The result of such a growing, moving faith is that we will bear spiritual fruit that the world will be able to feast on, and so become aware of God our Father and Jesus our King and Savior in us.**

Perhaps this sounds like hard work to you. No, it's not because God doesn't leave you alone to wrestle with it for one moment. **Romans 12:3 says that God has given each of us a measure of faith.** He equips you with the ability of His Holy Spirit in you. The moment you reveal to Him your willingness of heart and obedience, He is ready to do the rest of the work in you. Where your ability stops, God's grace, ability and mercy takes over through the working of His Spirit within you.

Now without faith it is impossible to please Him, for the one who approaches God
must believe that He exists
and that He rewards those who seek Him
Hebrews 11:6

"He replied, "What is impossible for mere humans is possible for God."
Luke 18:27

Abba Father, I confess my 100% dependence on You.
Without You, I am nothing and I cannot achieve anything meaningful.
I believe in You to do all that I want You to do according to Your will.
Let your Spirit instruct, guide, and validate me, that I may live to Your glory.
Thank You for hearing me.
in The Name of Jesus.
Amen.

MEASURE YOUR FAITH AGAINST APOSTOLIC TRUTH

Luke 6:13
'When morning came, he called his disciples and chose twelve of them,
<u>*whom He also named apostles:*</u>

Romans 10:8-10,17
"But what does it say? "The word is near you, in your mouth and in your heart"
(That is, the word of faith that we preach), because
if you confess with your mouth that Jesus is Lord and believe in your heart
that God raised Him from the dead, you will be saved.
For with the heart, one believes and thus has righteousness and
with the mouth one confesses and thus has salvation.
For the Scripture says, "Everyone who believes in Him will not be put to shame.
Consequently, faith comes from what is heard,
and what is heard comes through the preached word of Christ."

In the beginning of the book, under the topic **"Quality Communication between God & You** "we saw where the Apostles fitted into the "picture" of the life of Jesus, as well as in the time period after the ascension of Jesus to heaven.
In short, just a reminder:

- ❖ Jesus chose twelve disciples who later became His apostles. Luke 6:13
- ❖ Disciples are followers of Jesus who learned from Jesus to do His will accurately.
- ❖ Jesus teaches and demonstrates to them how to live according to His Gospel and what the truth is around this Gospel of Jesus Christ (which also involves the principles of God's Kingdom.)
- ❖ The word "Apostle" in Greek is "Apostlelo" (G652 & G649) which has the following meaning: "To be set apart and to be sent on a mission."
- ❖ In Matthew 10 and Luke 10, Jesus introduced the disciples to their mission as "sent ones."
- ❖ The Apostles carried out and lived according to the message of Jesus Christ and the principles of God's Kingdom accurately, as they were taught. So, they acted in Jesus' Name and were representatives/ambassadors of Jesus. Jesus goes so far as to say that if the apostles and their Gospel are rejected, the people reject Jesus. Read about it in Matthew 10:40.
- ❖ After Jesus ascended to heaven, the Apostles waited for the outpouring of the Holy Spirit that equipped them for the mission of Jesus Christ. Acts 1 and 2 describe these events.
- ❖ Next, we see the Apostles going out and fulfilling their mission. A multitude of congregations that identify with the pure Gospel of Jesus Christ are established. Of these we read in Acts and in the letters, Paul wrote to the various congregations.

Another important fact to keep in mind is the qualities of the Old and the New Testament Message. The central message of the <u>Old Testament</u> revolved around the practices of the law and carries the quality of between <u>RIGHT and WRONG</u> while the <u>New Testament</u> brings the fulfillment of the law through Jesus Christ and the establishment of the Commandment of Love and the law of the Spirit. The New Testament's central message is not law-bound, but more aimed <u>at TRUTH and LIE.</u> <u>LOVE</u> stands out as the essence of what Jesus wanted to convey through His Gospel in the New Testament.

The test for truth is not in how serious we are about what we believe. It is the content or detail of our faith that determines truth or lie. For illustration, we can look at the following situation: -

FAITH IN A LIE...

➤ Years ago, people believed the earth was flat and not round.
➤ Evidence was obtained that the Earth is round and this round globe hangs in space.
➤ Some people believed the "new" truth while others rejected it.
➤ Today, we still find people who believe in the lie that the earth is flat. They founded an organization called "The Flat Earth Society."

The Results of believing a lie – deceitful faith

It leads to inaccurate faith principles that remove people from God's Truth.

If NASA were to cling to the above belief of a flat Earth, while it is not true, it could lead to people getting lost in space, which could lead to the death of these people.

Similarly, the belief in spiritual lies can lead to error and deception that would eventually lead to the eternal death of those who adhere to the lie.

THE SOURCE OF THE MESSAGE ON WHICH FAITH IS BUILT
The False Messenger

People and spiritual leaders who bring a different message or modified message, **that deviates from the original true message, are false messengers**. Paul speaks of this in Galatians 1:6-7 where he says the following:

"I am astonished that you are so quickly deserting the one who called you by the grace of Christ and are following a different gospel – not that there really is another gospel, but there are some who are disturbing you and wanting to distort the gospel of Christ."

It is not the apostles or our responsibility to interpret the gospel by reading things into the Word of God that are not there.

In Matthew 24:24, Jesus describes these messengers as:

➤ False Prophets
➤ Wolves in Sheep's Clothing
➤ False Christians
➤ False Apostles

Today's challenge is to distinguish the true light of Jesus' message from darkness. Paul further warns in Galatians 1:8 with these words: **"But even if we or an angel from heaven should preach to you a gospel contrary to the one we preached to you, let him be accursed!"** and in 2 Corinthians 11:2-4 and verses 13-15, Paul warns the congregation to be cautious: **"For I am jealous over you with a godly jealousy, For I have bound you to one husband, that I may present you as a pure virgin to Christ. But I am afraid that, just as the serpent deceived Eve by his craftiness, so your minds may be corrupted from the sincerity toward Christ. For if anyone comes and preaches another Jesus than we have preached, or if you receive a spirit other than what you have received, or some other gospel that you have received, let it be well."** And verses 13-15 **"For such are false apostles, deceitful workers, transforming themselves into apostles of Christ. And no wonder! For Satan himself transforms himself into an angel of light. Therefore, it is no great way for his servants to masquerade as ministers of righteousness. But their end will be according to their works."**

One of the worrying facts of the day is that people nowadays gather for themselves preachers who caress their audience who in principle do not preach the accurate truth of Jesus Christ and His Apostles. That is why we need to be vigilant. We read about this in 2 Timothy 4:3-4: **"For** there will be a time when people will not tolerate sound teaching. Instead, following their own desires, they will accumulate teachers for themselves, because they have an insatiable curiosity to hear new things. And they will turn away from hearing the truth, but on the other hand they will turn aside to myth." Also Read 2 Timothy 3:1-8.

The truths of the Gospel of Jesus Christ, which was also the Gospel that the Apostles preached, are the very truth that we must adhere to in faith. It will require that we have the necessary knowledge and insight regarding this Evangelist so that we can talk about it with conviction.

The Messenger Who Carries and Preaches the Accurate Truth
True messengers take the responsibility of transmitting the message accurately as he/she received it, without adding or omitting anything that could distort the central accurate truth.

Such a messenger realizes that he/she is **not called to interpret it according to human thought**. The message must be brought as the Lord has truly said.
He/she realizes that the message does not belong to him/her.

Jesus is the center of what he/she preaches — no honor of his own.
A true Messenger's walk of life testifies to the One in whom he/she believes and whose message he/she carries.

CHARACTERISTICS OF TRUE AND FALSE MESSENGERS THAT HELP DISTINGUISH THE TYPE OF MESSENGER
True Messengers
We look at **JESUS' conduct in** John 7:16-18 and John 8:26b,28b,38:
- ❖ Here we see the outstanding qualities of a true messenger.
- ❖ Jesus does not bring His own formulated teaching or doctrine.
- ❖ His Word is not intended for those who misuse and distort His Word.
- ❖ He also does not manipulate others with His message. They must choose for themselves what they want to believe.
- ❖ Jesus does not speak for His own gain.
- ❖ He does not seek His own glory, but honors God the Father who gave the message. Jesus says that the test of integrity and justice is associated with what honor is sought.
- ❖ Jesus said nothing He didn't hear His Father say, nor did He do anything He didn't see His Father do. He is in dependence on His Father.
- ❖ Jesus also says that He does not come in His own Name, but in the Name of His Father – See John 5:43.
- ❖ In John 5:30, Jesus says he seeks not His own will, but the will of His Father who sent Him.
- ❖ Jesus goes so far as to say that if He testifies about Himself, His testimony is not true — see John 5:31.
- ❖ **Jesus Himself was identified as an Apostle**, since He was sent by His Father. Read about it in Hebrews 3:1. He had an earthly mission commissioned by His Father.

Holy Spirit as True Messenger — read John 16:13-15:
- ❖ The Holy Spirit does not speak of Himself.
- ❖ The Holy Spirit honors Jesus, not Himself.
- ❖ He does not honor any pastor or ministry.
- ❖ The Holy Spirit takes what belongs to Jesus and proclaims it.

Characteristics of a False Messenger
False Messengers Carry and are connected to False Spirits
➢ They speak from their own authority.
➢ False messengers have their own selfish interests in mind.
➢ They have no integrity or justice.
➢ Speaking of yourself, as a messenger, is proof of error even if you have an international ministry.
➢ Ask the question - In whose name does the messenger bring his message?
➢ Is the message in line with the Gospel of Jesus Christ and the principles of the Kingdom of God or not?

The **Spirit of the Antichrist** as Messenger
➢ He comes in his own name.
➢ He speaks on his own authority.
➢ He can quote many Scriptures but does not necessarily apply them correctly and within context. Satan did this with Jesus in His time of temptation in the wilderness.
➢ He distorts the accurate truth and misuses it to seduce people for their own gain.
➢ So, he preaches his own message, **not** the Gospel of Jesus Christ.

The Apostolic Truth
The **Apostolic truth was and is accurate in line with the Gospel of Jesus Christ. They acted according to the qualities of true messengers as Jesus taught them.**

Jesus sent them out with a heavenly mission based on His Gospel and the principles of the Kingdom of heaven. Please read Matthew 28:19 and Mark 16:15-18.

The Acts Church originated right after the outpouring of the Holy Spirit on the Apostles. **Their message was not their own, but that of Jesus Himself, deposited in their hearts by the Holy Spirit who has now come to make them His dwelling place and temple.**

We see how the new congregation of Acts in Acts 2 arises after being baptized in the Name of Jesus Christ, for the remission of sins, and they also receive the gift of the indwelling Holy Spirit. Outstanding qualities of the congregation were that they functioned on four spiritual pillars as we see in Acts 2:42: "**They were devoting themselves to the apostles' teaching and to fellowship, to the breaking of bread and to prayer.**"

They were **united** in what they believed as we see in Acts 2:46. Their faith became **a life of full - time worship.** Every day they went from house to house, practicing these four spiritual pillars as mentioned earlier. In verse 47, we see that they also praised the Lord during these house visits.

The Apostolic truth puts us purely within the teachings of the New Testament and New Covenant of Jesus Christ. And the old things have passed away. Please read this in Hebrews 8:8-13 and Hebrews 9:14-17. The Old Testament was a shadow of what was to come and was pointing to Jesus who was and is the answer and fulfillment of the Old Testament. He came and validated a New Testament with His death and resurrection. **One of the greatest truths Christians need to grasp is that we as Christians do not come from the Old Testament. We belong to Jesus Christ, who is the Author and Finisher of our faith.**

In John 8:31-32, Jesus says, "Jesus said to the Jews who believed in Him, '**If you abide in My Word, you are truly my disciples.' And you will know the truth, and the truth will set you free.**"

Herein lies the key to accurate belief in the truth of Jesus Christ, - that is, **to abide, meaning to live by and putting your faith in the Word of Jesus**. **Living and doing Jesus' Word brings freedom according to the Truth of Jesus' Word.**

Satan wants to rob us of the truth.
Therefore, we must be courageous.
The Truth of Jesus Christ and the Kingdom and
The Teachings of the Apostles
Should also be our mission
To live and proclaim,
We are called to know the truth of Jesus Christ.
Use it as a criterion for our faith.

... WHEN TRUE WORSHIPPERS WORSHIP THE FATHER IN SPIRIT AND TRUTH...

John 4:23-24
"But a time is coming – and now is here –
when the true worshippers will worship the Father in spirit and truth,
for the Father seeks such people to be His worshipers.
God is Spirit,
and the people who worship Him
must worship in spirit and truth."

When we read the events of that day at the well in John 4:1-30, it seems, to be just another piece of history from Jesus' earthly course of life. Yet there is a deeper meaning in it. For these spiritual discoveries, we will look at the background and circumstances of that time and examine the original Greek meanings of certain words so that we can gain insight into what Jesus really wanted to convey here.

This Samaritan woman was very much attuned to the perspectives and perceptions of that time:
- ❖ First, she is surprised that a Jew, namely Jesus, asks her for water to drink, since Jews and Samaritans did not mix or communicate with each other at all. (See John 4:9).
- ❖ Like the Jews, she did not recognize Jesus as the Messiah at all. (See John 4:10,12,22,25,26);
- ❖ When Jesus speaks of living water, she still thinks of physical water, not spiritual water. (See this John 4:15).
- ❖ When she speaks of worship, we see that she is focused on a physical place of worship and not on the possibility of another place of worship which might be of a spiritual nature. (See John 4: 20).

With this event, **Jesus is announcing a new way of life**:
1. He breaks down the man-made spiritual walls of lovelessness between Jew and Samaritan in recognition that this woman also has a human dignity within His perspective.
2. He offers her living water, even though she doesn't yet understand what He means; (See John 4: 10,13-15).
3. Jesus makes her aware of a more personal form of worship that was not the practice of those days (See John 4: 23,24).
4. Jesus also points out that the form and practice of worship must be one of spirit and truth and that God should be worshiped as Father (See John 4:23,24).
5. The woman's spiritual eyes are opened during the conversation, and she realizes that Jesus is the long-awaited Messiah! (See John 4:25,26).

THE DEEPER MESSAGE...
In John 4:10, 14-15, we read of the living waters Jesus gives us. **Water is symbolic of the Spirit inspired spoken Word of God.** In Jeremiah 2:13, we see that God describes Himself as a "fountain of living water." God is Spirit and His Spirit gives life as Jesus says in John 6:63: **"It is the Spirit that gives life; the flesh profits nothing; the words (G4487 = "rhema" = revealed word) that I speak to you are spirit and are life."**

It is this "living waters" that become a "fountain" that "springs up into eternal life" when we accept it and make it our own. It is the Holy Spirit who makes Jesus' gospel well up into our midst and overflows to the Glory of the Lord. Also, please read Ephesians 1:17-18 where we see that it is the <u>Holy Spirit who gives us insight and wisdom to understand the Word of God.</u>

The symbolic meaning of the "woman" can also be the **church of saved believers** (In Greek, the **"Ecclesia"**). The problem is that, like the woman, there is a section of the Ecclesia Church/Believers who are spiritually lacking in need of the necessary insight so that they can truly worship Abba Father in spirit and truth. It's a scary thought.

One of the most important spiritual challenges for the Ecclesia Church is the misrepresentation of the place of worship. Like the Jews and Samaritans, they cling to the perception that they must go to a physical place (building) of worship to meet with the Lord there.

In the **Old Testament**, it was the Tabernacle and Temple that was considered a place of worship, for the Lord's presence was in the Most Holy of the Tabernacle or Temple. It was perfectly right for that time period. It was <u>more focused on a form of corporate worship</u> where there was dancing, praying corporately, offering an animal sacrifice according to the law, and then the people were in anticipation of a message from the Lord via the High Priest. <u>The Holy Spirit descended upon some people, but this did not result in the indwelling of the Holy Spirit</u>. There are only a few instances where the filling of the Holy Spirit took place as with Gideon in Judges 6:16 - 34.

<u>In the **New Testament Era**, Jesus announces a new worship methodology</u>.
First, John the Baptist identifies Jesus as the One who will baptize with the Holy Spirit and fire, as defined in Matthew 3:11. We see the fulfillment of this in Acts 2 when the Apostles were baptized with the Holy Spirit. What we need to realize is that this baptism with the Holy Spirit also results in the **indwelling** of the Holy Spirit in the Apostles and every saved believer.
In 1 Corinthians 6:19-20 we read, "Do **you not know that your bodies are the temple of the Holy Spirit, which is <u>in</u> you, which you have of God,** and that you are not your own? **Because you were bought with a price. <u>Therefore, glorify God in your body and in your spirit,</u>** which **are God's.** " We read further in 2 Corinthians 6:16b-18: "... **For ye are the temple of the living God**, as God hath said, I **will dwell in them,** and **walk among them,** and I will be their God, and they shall be my people. Therefore, go out from among them, and separate yourselves, says the Lord. And touch not the unclean thing, and I will receive you. and I **will be a Father to you,** and **you shall be sons and daughters** to Me, **says the Lord Almighty**."

The third temple that enjoys so much attention in the news these days, currently seen as a concrete, physical building to be erected, is an inaccurate account of what the word of the Lord tells us. **Every saved (Ecclesia) believer's body is symbolically the third temple since the indwelling of the Holy Spirit is in their body and therefore, they do not have to seek out the Lord somewhere in a holy place or building.** The Lord is not far, somewhere there in space, no, **He is Spirit and therefore He can come and make a home in us**. This means that **we also carry with us the constant presence of the Lord** and thus have a **constant awareness in our heart and mind of Him. As a born again, saved believing child of God, we also have Him as Father in our lives, because we are His children.**

Jesus says to the woman at the well of water in John 4:23-24: ""**But a time is coming – and now is here – when the true worshipers will worship the Father in spirit and truth, for the Father seeks such people to be his worshipers. God is Spirit, and the people who worship Him, must worship in spirit and truth.**"

Jesus first indicates the time period— "... **And it is now**..."it still includes today!

Who are the **"true worshippers"**? The original Greek meaning for "true" indicates "truthfulness" and **"worshippers"** in G4353 and G4352 indicates in Greek as translated into

English, to "adorer." Thus, **being a true worshipper involves a personal spirit of truth and an honest admiration of the One you worship.** The Lord knows the motive of our heart and can thus determine how genuine our worship really is.

"Spirit" in Biblical perspective according to G4151 is **"pneuma"** which denotes **"a current of air that is breath or breeze."** Here we see that **our spirit should actually be in a constant state of worship, with every breath we take.**

"Truth" also involves the condition of our heart.

When we look at the word **"worship"** in the Greek language, we learn how we should admire the Lord. **"Worship** "is explained in G4352, G4314, and G2965, and the Greek word is "proskuneo" which means **"to kiss like a dog licking his master's hand, or crouch or to prostrate oneself in homage and in reverence and adoration in worship action."** In other words, worship isn't just a slow song after a few quick songs. This doesn't include a "show" with lights and great musical instruments and singers, which I sing with in church. **Worship involves a way of life in which our spirit worships Abba Father with every breath you and I take, in truth.** The awareness that God is constantly within me through His Spirit influences every decision, deed, and walk so that everything is done for The Glory of His name.

We can conclude from John 4's events and the Samaritan woman's answers to Jesus that the people did not worship God as Father at that time. We see that Jesus is constantly speaking of **"the Father"** and that as Father **He is looking for people who will worship him in spirit and truth.** Here, too, a "key" to worship is given, namely, **that we worship God as our Father. If we see ourselves as born again, saved believing children of God, He is our Father.** We need to build a deeper faith around this fact so that we can appropriate it for ourselves.

As I said earlier, the "woman" is a type/depiction of the Church. The question we actually have to ask ourselves today is what does the church's "worship fruit" really look like? What is the detail of the activities of the worship program? First a "Nice" song to make myself feel good; or do I do it for the experience of self-honor, not to honor God? Who or what is the focus point of what is being done during worship? Are we going to seek God's presence at church? Is this accurate in line with what the Ecclesia church did in Acts and in the New Testament? Is this what Jesus is teaching us about worship?

We need to reflect prayerfully on this according to the principles of the Word of Jesus and the Apostles in the New Testament, for this is where we will find the answers.

Jesus actually spoke of an "internal" form of worship in John 4:23-24, that's why He says in "spirit and truth." He's talking about your spirit, here.

Old Testament worship was directed outward because God's glory was still external. After Jesus' coming on earth, His resurrection from the dead and Ascension to Heaven, the glory of God is within the Ecclesia/saved believer and therefore worship should be directed inwardly. As explained earlier, Jesus came to dwell within us, meaning His Spirit in us is present in our body which is now the temple of God.

In Ephesians 5:19-20 We read: " Speaking to one another in psalms, hymns, and spiritual songs, singing and making music **in your hearts to the Lord** always giving thanks to God the Father for each other in the Name of our Lord Jesus Christ." Colossians 3:16 explains a similar concept: "Let the word of Christ dwell in you richly, teaching and exhorting one another with all wisdom, singing psalms, hymns, and spiritual songs, **all with grace in your hearts to God**."

Here we see a dual form of worship that begins with the inner experience with the Lord, namely that when the **word of Jesus dwells richly in you,** it will **overflow into personal worship** beginning with praises and psalms and songs of thanks in **your heart** and as a result it will **bubble over like a fountain into corporate worship in the form** of fellowship with fellow saved believers in the form of "speaking and exhorting one another with psalms, songs of praise and spiritual songs.

Jesus remains the focus point of this entire worship practice with the words in these verses saying
   "... **giving thanks to God the Father for all things in the Name of our Lord Jesus Christ" and "... in honor of the Lord."**

When we look at the first **New Testament congregation** in Acts 2:42,46,47, which were taught by the Apostles of Jesus Christ, we see their worship practices were as follows:
- ❖   "And they **continued steadfastly in the teaching of the apostles,** and
- ❖   **in the fellowship** and
- ❖   **in the breaking of bread**, and
- ❖   **in prayers**.
- ❖   **Every day they continued with one accord in the temple, breaking bread from house to house,** enjoying their food **with joy** and **humbleness of heart,**
- ❖   **praising God** and having the good will of the people.
And the Lord added to the church daily those who were being saved."

However, we should not neglect the gatherings of the faithful, for it is during these meetings that believers can establish and build each other up as described above.

Jesus' words in John 4 from verses 13-14 to 23-24
are the definition of true worship in terms of
the Kingdom of heaven.
Let us not disregard it but practice it
to glorify and worship the Lord and
to build up our love relationship with Him.

"...BUT YOU, WHENEVER YOU PRAY..."

Matthew 6:6
"But whenever you (New Testament believer) pray, go into your room, close the door, and pray to your Father in secret. And your Father, who sees in secret, will reward you."

We are often so inclined to see only the superficial value of the Bible and not look deeper at what the Lord actually wants to say to us. Never did I think I would discover in the deep meaning of prayer that Jesus meant much more than we generally define as prayer.

In the **Old Testament era** prayer was directed outwardly, because God's glory in, for example., the Most Holy of the Tabernacle or Temple was either because His glory was visible in the pillar of fire and pillar of cloud. Read about this in Exodus 13:21-22 and Exodus 40:34-35. At other times His glory was visible on Mount Sinai, and when Moses came down from the mountain, God's glory was visible on Moses' face, and he had to wear a covering because Israel could not look at him. Also read about this in Exodus 24:17-18. God's glory was almost palpable due to its visible manifestation. When the people prayed, they often did so in outward display, somewhere where they were visible to others.

When you look at Jesus' prayer life, you will see that His teaching about prayer and His application of it were in harmony with one another. Nowhere do we see that Jesus has publicly made a great show of His prayer life. The times He prayed publicly was to give thanks to His heavenly Father in recognition of food as with the increase of the loaves and fish, given to the multitude of people. In most cases, we read how Jesus isolated Himself early in the morning or late at night by going out on the mountain to pray. We see one such event in Mark 1:35; "Now early **in the morning, still deep in the night,** he got up and went out **to a lonely place** and prayed **there.** "

As mentioned earlier in the previous writing on worship in John 4:23-24 Jesus announced a deeper form of worship that also joins to prayer.
Jesus further expands this phenomenal change around prayer when we read **Matthew 6:5-7:**
" **Whenever you pray, do not be like the hypocrites, because they love to pray while standing in synagogues and on street corners so that people can see them. Truly I say to you, they have their reward. But whenever you pray, go into your room, close the door, and pray to your Father in secret. And your Father, who sees in secret, will reward you. When you pray, do not babble repetitiously like the Gentiles, because they think that by their many words they will be heard."**

This phenomenal change in prayer methodology is because of the fact that God's glory shifted from the Ark of the Covenant in the Tabernacle/Temple to the spirit of the faithful in the **New Testament era**. This perception was difficult for the Jews, Pharisees, and experts in the law to grasp because they had not yet understood the change that God Himself had brought. They were still trapped in their legalistic perceptions in which their righteous, impressive works, according to people's opinions, would bring them into heaven and eternal life.

Let's look at Jesus' words in Matthew 6:5-6.
"And when you **pray**....
When you look at the Greek wording for the word "pray," here, one gets a revelation.
"Pray" = G4336, which in Greek is "proseuchomai". This word's real meaning is **WORSHIP.** It is not "arya" (G685) found in other passages of Scripture and which has the meaning of "a prayer

as lifted to Heaven." Nor is it "stenazo" (G4727) that means to pray out of necessity — a cry for help.

We see the same meaning for "praying" in Mark 1:35 where Jesus goes to pray alone in the early morning **which is "worship"**.
Jesus says in Matthew 6:5 "... **When you pray**" which is "**worship**" in true meaning,
➢   "Do not be as the hypocrites..." You don't have to be like an actor.
➢   "For they love to stand and pray in the synagogues and on the corners of the streets..."
         It's an outward display.
➢   "To be seen by these people." It was their real motive of the heart that Abba Father had
         observed. This type of conduct was more self-honoring than to honor God.
➢   "Truly I say to you that they have their reward." The word "reward" is also seen as "a
         wage" in this regard which adds to the meaning "the payment for services rendered". So,
         there is no heavenly price of compensation.

These kinds of prayers are carnal and artificial. That's not what Abba Father is looking for. We can say it so easily, but I don't do it that way. Well, think of the prayer practices within the modern church. The lady prayer hours, the different forms of corporate prayers etc. is often the place where the pain and sorrow of others are exposed and discussed in a different way rather than praying in all sincerity about it. **Corporate prayer in the right perspective is not wrong**, but often the prayers in such situations are not in line with Abba Father's expectation.

Our answer isn't another show, no, it's time for seclusion —"**go into your room and lock the door**" also known as "**your secret closet...**"
True worship (prayer as stated in this context of the Passage by Jesus) is in spirit (your spirit) and truth (sincerity - "truthfulness") of the heart, within the third temple, which means your body where the Spirit of the Lord has taken occupancy, where God's glory is now present. Jesus speaks to the Jews and tells them, "Tear down this temple and in three days I will raise it up." John 2:19. Again, the Jews misunderstood this, for their perspective was directed at the concrete physical temple building, while Jesus spoke of His body. We see this in verse 21, where it is written, "**But He spoke of the temple of His body.**"
Even before Jesus' death, Jesus began to point out the "new place of worship", namely, that your spirit and body become the temple of God as defined in 1 Corinthians 6:19-20 <u>**"Do you not know that your bodies are the temple of the Holy Spirit, which is in you, which you have of God, and that you do not belong to yourselves? Because you were bought with a price. Therefore, glorify God in your body (and in your spirit,) which are God's."**</u>

Building another physical, concrete temple building in Jerusalem is, in fact, another deception to lead the people of Abba Father away to a deceitful form of religion.

<u>In Matthew 6:6, Jesus says...</u>
➢   "... **Pray to your Father who is <u>in secret</u>**. Abba Father is only "visible" to those who
         seek Him in isolation.
➢   "... and **see you in secret...**" He sees you there praying and worshipping in private.
➢   "... **You will <u>be rewarded openly</u>.**" It is Abba Father's choice to repay you. It's not
         subject to people's opinions.
The hidden meaning for "in secret" in Greek (G2927) "concealed, private: - hidden, **inward secret.** In other words, inner secrecy — just between you and your heavenly Father...
It is this kind of prayer/worship that will be answered.

We see that there have been times of corporate prayer in the Acts Church. We read about it in

Acts 1:14 and Acts 4:24-31. In Acts 1:14, we see that the word "pray" can also be interpreted as worship from the Greek words used there. In Acts 4:31, the word "pray" is conveyed differently in the Greek with the meaning of petitioning and making supplication to the Lord.

What we need to realize is that the form of corporate prayer has been practiced differently than in the modern context of today. It was not one who prayed and the other said "Amen." No boasting prayers were prayed. Each prayed aloud, simultaneously, while they were personally directed at Abba Father, but they prayed for the same subject. That is why there was absolute unity.

Jesus teaches us in Matthew 6:9-13 how to pray.
"Our Father which art in heaven, Hallowed be Thy name.
Thy kingdom comes. Thy will be done in earth, as it is in heaven.
Give us this day our daily bread.
And forgive us our debts, as we forgive our debtors.
And lead us not into temptation, but deliver us from evil:
For thine is the kingdom, and the power, and the glory, forever.
Amen. "

In this prayer many spiritual treasures can be discovered. One thing is certain, it is not a long request list and "orders" addressed to our Heavenly Father. God Himself is glorified in this prayer and He will provide as He promised, for your heavenly Father knows what things you need.

There is much more to prayer to examine and discover from the pure truth of the Bible. Begin to examine for yourself and discover the heavenly treasures that Abba Father has for you.

When We Follow Jesus' Instructions and Example,
Prayer and worship will
result in wonderful miraculous moments
from our Abba Father's heart.

FOR OUT OF THE ABUNDANCE OF THE HEART
THE MOUTH SPEAKS

Matthew 12:33-37
"Make a tree good and its fruit will be good,
or make a tree bad and its fruit will be bad,
for a tree is known by its fruit.
Offspring of vipers! How are you able to say anything good, since you are evil?
For the mouth speaks from what fills the heart.
The good person brings good things out of his good treasury,
and the evil person brings evil things out of his evil treasury.
I tell you that on the day of judgment,
people will give an account for every worthless word they speak.
For by your words, you will be justified, and
by your words you will be condemned."

When we look at this passage in context, we see the Church leaders, the experts in the law and Pharisees of that time going out of their way to pursue Jesus and find fault with everything He does and speaks.

The chapter begins with His hungry disciples picking wheat ears on the Sabbath to eat. After that, Jesus heals a man's withered hand, followed up with the casting out of demons from a man who was blind, dumb, and devil possessed. Even this man was healed too. With all these practices, the church leaders found fault. They are so caught up in the law that they are also spiritually blind themselves, focusing on the so-called obedient works of the law and completely forgot the love commandment which requires a continuous conduct of love.

With such a CV, one cannot imagine that they continuously declared so much negative words of criticism toward Jesus. They not only hated what Jesus did and preached but plotted to kill Jesus as seen in Matthew 12:13-14.

After Jesus delivers the demon-possessed man from demons and heals him, the Pharisees and church leaders insult and blaspheme the Holy Spirit by implying that Jesus performed these miracles through Beelzebub (Satan). See this in Matthew 12:24.

After all the undeserved criticism and commentary, Jesus says in Matthew 12:33: "Make a tree good and its fruit will be good or make a tree bad and its fruit will be bad, for a tree is known by its fruit .... **For the mouth speaks from what fills the heart**. The KJV says it somewhat otherwise, but it carries the same message: "... **out of the abundance of the heart the mouth speaks.**

Here man is symbolically compared to trees that will bear fruit. The underlying message of what Jesus said here, is where the tree was planted and what characteristics the tree has according to its DNA (genetic material that determines identity).
Colossians 2:6-7 says: "**Therefore, just as you received Christ Jesus as Lord, continue to live your lives in Him, rooted and built up in Him and firm in your faith** just as you were taught, and overflowing with thankfulness." First of all, it is our choice that we need to make, to determine in whose footsteps we want to follow. Here we are advised, after we have received Jesus, to walk in Him and be rooted and built up in Him. Our spiritual DNA (genetic material) will therefore be according to Jesus' will and practices. We receive our spiritual DNA in the likeness of God the moment we choose to invite Jesus into our heart and life resulting into being born again. That, which will then flow from our heart and mouth, will be words for the glory of

Jesus' Name and not criticism. Being built up in Him means spending enough time with the Bible so that we will speak and live spiritually in line with His Word, Gospel, and Kingdom principles. We will also walk in love as Jesus teaches us. We need to maintain our relationship with Him by being rooted and built up in His Word.

The Pharisees were aware of the love commandment but did not practice it at all as Jesus recommended. For them, it was just words. To them, the law was a "rod" with which they could "beat" and criticize and defame people so that they felt they would never make heaven. Their misperceptions kept them from what God really wanted to give them and offered them.

In John 8:42-44, Jesus says to them: ""**If God were your Father, you would love Me, for I have come from God** and am now here. **I have not come on My own initiative, but He sent Me.** Why don't you understand what I am saying? It is because you cannot accept my teaching. **You people are from your father, the devil, and you want to do what your father desires. He was a murderer from the beginning**, and does not uphold the truth, because there is no truth in him. **Whenever he lies, he speaks according to his own nature**, because he is a liar and the father of lies."
 With these statements, Jesus identifies the spiritual DNA of church leaders, the experts of the law, and Pharisees, **pointing out that the fruit they bear is in harmony with who their father is and what his desires are, in whom they are rooted.**

Each of us needs to reflect on what comes out of our mouths, because it reveals what kind of "trees" we are, what fruit we bear, in whom we are rooted, and what spiritual DNA is inherent in our heart and spirit. We so often stop ourselves with negative criticisms, insults, and comments that in principle affect ourselves as well.
We so easily say:
"I can't help getting angry so easily — it runs in the family; my dad was like that...."
"Her mother has cancer and heart disease; she's going to get it too."
"My husband/wife is so bad, he/she will never change!"
"The child is so stupid; he will never pass matric."
"My marriage is so unhappy. I think divorce is the only option."
"He/she is a hopeless case. We can forget, I think he/she has no chance for improvement."
"I'm sure he is possessed, otherwise he wouldn't have acted that way!"
"Everybody coughs and sneezes like that. It's probably COVID's fault. I'm probably going to get sick, too."
"I'll never forgive him for what he did to me, I hate him for it!"

We are so inclined to make negative statements — often without thinking about what we're actually doing or saying right now, especially when we're angry.   In our negativity, we convince ourselves that this is a hopeless matter. We accept the negative "facts" that life throws at us: addiction, disappointments, unhappy marriage, persistent adversity, COVID pandemic etc. and sit down in doubt and despair.

What we often lose sight of is what is stated in the following passage:
Romans 10:17 says:
"So, then **faith comes by hearing**, and **hearing by the word of God.**"
While this is a very positive statement, the opposite is also true.
When we **speak negative, critical words, the faith around those words is also generated** as we hear ourselves. In our brains, nerve networks with the same message in the form of DNA (genetic material), are stored in those nerve networks. They, in turn give commands to our body and also to those that hear it. The negative or positive statements can therefore have a profound negative or positive impact on our body.

It is in view of this, that Solomon says in Proverbs 18:21: **"Death and life are in the power of the tongue; And everyone who loves to use it will eat its fruit**."
In this way, what you confess with your mouth carries spiritual strength that can positively or negatively affect you and other **people.**

Please read the following Scriptures: -
Proverbs 15:1-2 – **"A gentle response turns away anger. The tongue of the wise treats knowledge correctly**, but the mouth of the fool spouts out folly.
Proverbs 18:4-8 – **Anger has the power to result in your destruction.**
Proverbs 12:18,19 – The **power of careless words brings emotional pain** into another person's heart, but the power of wise words brings **healing.**
Proverbs 15:28; Proverbs 10:11,19,21 The **righteous man's tongue brings forth life** and is filled **with wisdom.**
1 Timothy 6:20 and 2 Timothy 2:15,16,17a - **Nonsensical, unholy talk draws you away from God. It leads to the destruction of your faith and hope in God.**
Revelation 12:10,11; Revelation 3:5 - We **overcome by the** Word of Our Testimony.
James 3 spells out the influence of the spoken word. In the end of the chapter James said: **"But the wisdom from above is first pure, then peaceable, gentle, accommodating, full of mercy and good fruit, impartial, and not hypocritical. And the fruit that consists of righteousness is planted in peace among those who make peace."**
Jesus warns us in Matthew 12:36-37 with these words: "But I say to you that of every vein word (G692 and G2041, the Greek word is argos" which means "negative particles, useless" in this case, words) that the people speak, of which they must account for on judgment day.
For by thy words thou shalt be justified, and by thy words thou shalt be condemned."

We're going to **be accountable for the empty, idle, worthless words we've spoken.**

THEREFORE: -
❖ Don't make careless statements with your mouth.
❖ Your words bring forth the manifestation of a spirit — whether good or bad.
❖ God's Word is accomplished by His Spirit.
❖ Along with positive confessions, faith and hope become the driving force toward fulfilling our confessions, if they align with Abba Father's will.
❖ When we confess the Word of God, it generates faith in our hearts as Romans 10:9&17 tells us.

Examples of positive Word confession in the Bible and the results:
What did Jesus do when Satan came to him with his lies?
He repeatedly said, "It is written..." Matthew 4:1-11 Jesus confesses the Word along with the belief in His heart and it becomes the powerful "weapon" against Satan's temptations.
What did **Abraham** *do in faith for 25 years when God promised him a seed?*
He believed against hope and eventually experienced its fulfillment. Romans 4:18-20 Along with his faith, came his confession with which he clung to God's promise.
What did King **Jehoshaphat's** *language look like in the midst of crisis?*
Read 2 Chronicles 20:1,4-9,14,15,18,21-22,26
He reminded himself of the wonders and victories the Lord had given and brought in the past to establish his own faith and the faith of the people and confessed his faith in God. It became a form of praise that once again resulted in wonders from God's hand.
What language did the **spies of Canaan** *speak?*
Numbers 13:16,27-33; Numbers 14:6-9,23,24
The negative confession aroused unbelief among all the people, and they received the punishment of the Lord. In contrast, Joshua and Caleb positively confessed in faith that victory in the Lord's power was possible and they entered into the promised land.

Be careful what you confess with your mouth by keeping the following in mind: -
- ❖ Confession to the Lord – we ask forgiveness and need to receive it when given.
- ❖ Ask for forgiveness from others when needed. It brings restoration both to you and the other party's spirit and mind.
- ❖ Make an effort to drench yourself in the Word so that it positively affects our actions and conduct.
- ❖ Ask God to put a guard in front of your mouth.
- ❖ Take your mind captive to obedience to Christ Jesus.
- ❖ Exercise Obedience + Faith + Hope in the Lord.
- ❖ Think before you speak.

Divine equipment for a positive language use
*Realize and confess **your position** in Jesus Christ*
- ❖ Romans 8:14-15 We are adopted children of God and heirs with Jesus.
- ❖ 2 Corinthians 6:18 God is our Father, and He calls us His sons and daughters.
- ❖ 1 Peter 2:9 We are part of a chosen royal priesthood.
- ❖ Isaiah 43:1 God says that you are His.
- ❖ Romans 8:37 You are more than a conqueror.
- ❖ Believe it and live by it.
- ❖ *Jesus also gave* us His **_authority._**
  Read about it in Luke 10:19 and Matthew 10:7,8.

*Jesus' mission is to **bless instead.**
Matthew 5:44 Bless even your enemy.
Luke 10:5-6,10-11 Speak peace, do not curse.
Hebrew for peace is Shalom, which means prosperity in every part of a person's life.

Let's pray as David prayed:
"Lord, set a watchman before my mouth, keep the door of my lips."
Psalm 141:3.

BE TRANSFORMED BY THE RENEWING OF YOUR MIND

Romans 12:2
"And be not conformed to this world:
but be ye transformed by the renewing of your mind,
that you may prove what is that good,
and acceptable, and perfect, will of God."

In today's world of secular religion, there is a tendency to believe that if you repented and were born again, your path to heaven is paved. You don't have to do anything else. You don't have to change your lifestyle. You can continue with your old habits and when you pray or call on the Lord to do something for you, He will do it — almost like a Christmas father who just dispenses gifts as the children request.
       BUT....
What does Abba Father say in His Word about this?

John 1:12-13 says: "But to all who have received Him – those who believe in His Name – He has given the **right to become God's children**– children not born of human parents or by human desire or a husband's decision, **but by God**.

The word **"become"** in this verse is a key word to the true meaning of this verse. It's a word that doesn't point to a completed action, but rather points to a progressive action. It's an action that stays in motion and therefore isn't finished in that context.

Although you have established your position in Jesus Christ, it does not stop at that. There is something more that should happen, which is described in Romans 12:1-2: "Therefore I exhort you, brothers and sisters, by the mercies of God, to **present your bodies as a sacrifice – alive, holy, and pleasing to God –** which is your reasonable service. **Do not be conformed to this present world, but be transformed by the renewing of your mind, so that you may test and approve what is the will of God – what is good and well-pleasing and perfect.**

Our world of thought is constantly bombarded with words and thoughts from various sources. This includes positive and negative thoughts that are constantly being used by us as they run through our minds. We are constantly making choices whether we accept them or not. In general, many of these thoughts are self-focused, and often self-degrading. It's a self-centered existence that is about the satisfaction of myself. We reason on how others handle **us**. We keep our minds occupied with the world's things and allow things like the TV, Pornography, social media, gossip, etc. influence our thoughts to the point where they form our perceptions and opinions. In this way, we allow our mind to align with worldly practices that lead us away from our heavenly Father and His will for us. Many of us say we don't have time. No time for a daily special appointment with Jesus. What we need to realize is that what keeps us occupied will determine our conduct and way of life." It's called garbage in garbage out." We need to reflect on what we allow to shape our principles and perceptions in life and what we focus on in life, especially after we accept Jesus.

In Ephesians 4:21-24 Paul gives us the following advice: "
"If indeed you heard about Him and were taught in Him, just as the truth is in Jesus. You were taught with reference to your former way of life to **lay aside the old man** who is being corrupted in accordance with deceitful desires, **to be renewed in the spirit of your mind, and to put on the new man who has been created in God's image – in righteousness and holiness** that comes from truth."

In context, Paul is reproving the Ephesian congregation regarding the fact that they have fallen back into their old way of life (which he identifies as the "old man") after they accepted Jesus.

We see Paul giving several more commands in Scripture concerning the renewal of the congregations' (Ecclesia church -true saved believers) minds that would result in living according to Godly principles:
- ❖ Colossians 3:9-10 – Lay down the old man and clothe yourself with the new man.
- ❖ Colossians 3:1-2 Do not consider the things of the world but consider the things above.
- ❖ Romans 8:13 You must lay down the works of the flesh.
- ❖ 1 John 4:18 Be perfect in love and dispel fear that makes you give in to peer pressure.
- ❖ 1 Thessalonians 4:3-7 – Practice living in sanctification driven, and guided by the Spirit of Abba Father in our lives.

HOW DO WE APPLY THIS ADVICE IN OUR LIVES?
When we look at Romans 12:2's in-depth meaning, we see the following facts that bring us to the spiritual path that leads to this change/renewal.
"And be **not conformed** to this world: **but be transformed by the renewing of your mind,** that you may prove what is that good, and acceptable, and perfect, will of God."

"**Conformed**" in the Greek language, in G4964 means "**to fashion alike; to the same pattern of...**" Which then confirms that we should not be equivalent to the world's practices.
"**Transformed**" in the Greek translation in G3339 is known as "**metamorphosis.**"
It means that we must essentially, as in the scientific terminology, allow Abba Father to change us through the working of His Spirit so that we will live in line with God's will.
Per illustration, we can think of the caterpillar spinning itself into a cocoon and over a period of isolation, he is transformed into a beautiful butterfly. This whole process is called a "**metamorphosis**".

WHAT DOES A SPIRITUAL METAMORPHOSIS LOOK LIKE?
Transformation is **not** a process where we only exchange our fleshly works for spiritual works. It is the internal replacement of our sinful nature through the working of the Holy Spirit in our whole being — spirit and soul, after which the flesh/body will follow in obedience. Within the God given concept, it is the spirit that dictates the soul and the body how to act or live. It is our spirit that functions in submission to the Holy Spirit.

Titus 3:4-7 says the following:
"But when the kindness of God our Savior and His love for mankind appeared, **He saved us** not by works of righteousness that we have done, but on the basis of His mercy, **through the washing of the new birth and the renewing of the Holy Spirit,** whom He poured out on us in full measure through Jesus Christ our Savior. And so, since we have been justified by His grace, we become heirs with the confident expectation of eternal life."
In these verses we see that the first step in this process of renewal and of becoming a child of God, is to be baptized, which is in association with Jesus' death and resurrection into the new spiritual birth of being born again. You can also read more of it in Romans 6:3-6. This process also implies a "washing process" through the Spirit filled Word of God. This means that the Word of God generates the renewal and transformation of our mind, as we hear it and read it during which the Holy Spirit gives us the applicable insight into it.

Our spiritual DNA is renewed or regenerated through the workings of the Holy Spirit. Nothing you or I do, can bring about righteousness within us except Jesus Himself, who, through His Spirit works it in us. Please read John 3:5-6 again.

1 Peter 1:23 points out that we are born again from incorruptible seed and that that incorruptible seed is the spoken living Word of God. It is written as follows: "**You have been**

born anew, not from perishable but from <u>imperishable seed, through the living and enduring Word of God</u>.'
Each seed carries a unique DNA composition that determines its identity. In this context, it is the DNA that connects us to Jesus, and it originates from the living Word of God that begins to activate the renewal process in our minds as well.

The second step, which will surely go on for life, is the <u>renewal of the MIND — your THOUGHTS. This can only happen through meditation and study of the Word of God</u>. We must **constantly keep in mind that we are in fact a spirit with a soul that lives in a body.** Regeneration through being born again, produces the renewing of the spirit of man. The soul of man consists of the mind/thoughts, "understanding" through which we can gain insight, our willpower with which we make choices and decisions, and our emotions/feelings, among other things.

James 1:21-22 explains the renewing of the soul as follows: "So put away all filth and evil excess and humbly **welcome the <u>message implanted within you</u>, which is <u>able to save your souls</u>.** But be sure you live out the message and do not merely listen to it and so deceive yourselves. In other words, it is the "implanted Word of God" that renews our soul as God's Spirit gives us the necessary insight and conviction. It also generates the necessary faith in our hearts.

DAILY CHOICES....
In 1 Peter 1:13-15, Peter wrote:
"Wherefore **gird up the loins of your mind**, be sober, and hope to the end for the grace that is to be brought unto you at the revelation of Jesus Christ; <u>**As obedient children, not fashioning yourselves according to the former lusts in your ignorance:**</u> But as He which hath called you is holy, **<u>so be ye holy</u>** in all manner of conversation;"

In other words, Peter here uses similar typology as he speaks of the spiritual armor, as Paul did in Ephesians 6 when he said **"gird up your loins with the belt/girdle of Truth..."** What truth? **It is the Truth of the Gospel of Jesus Christ that was also the doctrine of the Apostles.** Peter takes it a small step further by saying that **this Truth should gird up our thinking.** We must drench our minds and thoughts with this truth by making time to read the Word of the Lord, studying the Bible correctly as discussed under the passage "Communication with God."

DETERMINE WHAT OR WHO CONTROLS YOUR MIND AND THINKING
Ephesians 4:23 says:
"To be <u>renewed in the spirit of your mind</u>, and to **put on the new man who has been created in God's image – in righteousness and holiness that comes from truth.** The **"spirit of your mind"** indicates your **attitude and motive with which you make your choices.** The word **"mind"** is also indicative of the intellect, will, and emotions that influence our understanding and insight.**

<u>James 4:3</u> points out that if you have wrong motives in your heart that are self-centered, you will receive no blessing via your prayer life. It is **important to regularly self-examine to determine the source of your motives and thoughts, because this ultimately determines your behavior.**
The Word of the Lord is the standard by which we must measure our perceptions and conduct, as defined in James 1:22-24. James explains how we see ourselves in the mirror of the Word of the Lord. We need to choose to replace our wrong perceptions with the Truth of the Gospel of Jesus Christ or not. In verse 25, James says that we need deep insight into the "perfect law of liberty" and must then abide by it in word and deed. We should not be forgetful about the Word.

It takes self-discipline by making purposeful decisions and actions to do so.

Colossians 3:1-2 reminds us to consider the things of above, where Jesus Christ is.

In Romans 8:5-6, Paul says: "For those who live according to the flesh have their outlook shaped by the things of the flesh, but **those who live according to the Spirit have their outlook shaped by the things of the Spirit.** For the outlook of the flesh is death, but the outlook of the Spirit is life and peace, because the outlook of the flesh is hostile to God, for it does not submit to the law of God, nor is it able to do so. **Those who are in the flesh cannot please God."**

As children of God, we should consider the things of the Spirit.

It is in the process of thinking about the Truth of the Gospel of Jesus Christ, that the renewing of our mind takes place. The word "meditating" in Biblical context, also includes, among other things, exercising your thinking in the Truth of the Gospel of Jesus Christ and His Word.

WHAT THE RESULTS OF MEDITATING ON THE WORD OF THE LORD?

David writes in Psalm 1 that the man who finds his delight in the law (Divine Principles) of the Lord and meditates on it day and night is very happy. **"He will be like a tree planted by streams of water, that gives its fruit in its season, and whose leaves do not wither; And he succeeds (prospers) in everything he attempts."**

Herein is a major spiritual key to rewriting your mind's DNA/genetic material in your brain that will determine your conduct and walk in life:

When we meditate on the fundamentals and principles of the Word of the Lord, day, and night, it has a positive impact on our entire life as it is engraved in our brain cells' DNA, throughout the process of protein synthesis and transcription. It impacts our conduct and walk in life, resulting in prosperity, and makes our lives God-blessed.

Why does David compare it to a tree? Isn't this by implication referring to the positive nerve network that looks like a dense green forest that forms in our minds?

The (nerve network) tree is planted at the streams of water, implying the impact and influence of the Holy Spirit inspired Word of the Lord. The tree grows because of the Holy Spirit inspired Word of God which is its source of nutrients (living waters) to develop into a healthy fruitful tree.

When we fall into negative thinking patterns, we are sinning, since those patterns of thinking are strongholds against the knowledge of God, as defined in 2 Corinthians 10:4,5 which says: **"for the weapons of our warfare are not human weapons but are made powerful by God for tearing down strongholds. We tear down arguments and every arrogant obstacle that is raised up against the knowledge of God, and we take every thought captive to make it obey Christ.".** In fact, it requires a little "self-talk" and washing with the Word of God as defined in Ephesians 5:26: "**That he might sanctify and cleanse it with the washing of water by the Word"**

When we meditate on the Word of God, as, for example, on **Philippians 4:8** "Finally, brothers and sisters, whatever **is true, whatever is worthy of respect, whatever is just, whatever is pure, whatever is lovely, whatever is commendable, if something is excellent or praiseworthy, think about these. "** and we choose to do it out of free choice, there are positive nerve "trees"/networks starting to form in our brains, which then secrete positive chemicals (hormones), such as serotonin, endorphins, enkephalin and dopamine, which make you feel good and bring feelings of calm, peace, love, and joy, and then result in healing and increased intellect.

Furthermore, the washing by the Word of God over the negative strongholds ("strongholds") in our minds is the double-edged sword that destroys the "thornbush nerve network" and forms new positive "nerve forest/networks" to heal the physical and psychological state of man.

So, in Psalm 103:3-5 David was able to "praise the Lord.... Who <u>forgives all your iniquities, who heals all your diseases,</u> who saves <u>your life from destruction,</u> who crowns you with lovingkindness and mercies, who <u>satisfies your soul with good things, so that your youth is renewed</u> like the eagle's."
By singing praises to God, describing His wonderful works, a detoxification process of our thinking patterns is activated, but at the same time a cut-off process of wrong thinking patterns and perceptions also follows!

Remember that **renewing the DNA, (which is embedded in your nerve network,) of your mind is a constant process,** joining hands with the **Sanctification Process,** which takes place **under the guidance of the Holy Spirit**. It's a lifelong process. As already explained, renewing the mind is a process that can only take place through constant meditation on, and exposure to the Word of the Lord, during quality time with the Lord. This meditation is different from the occultist forms of meditation where you "empty" your mind and, in fact, become receptive to the deceitful lies of evil. **Abba Father's prescription for meditation is precisely the opposite - to fill yourself with His Word under "rhema" revelation of His Spirit.**

This is of utmost importance because **the Free Will Center must be renewed by the Word of God so that we can become synonymous with God's will and thus become more sensitive to the guidance of the Holy Spirit that keeps us in line with God's will.** This results in **Psalm 37:4 becoming** a reality in our lives, namely, that the Lord will fulfill the desires of our hearts.

"But seek ye first the kingdom of God,
and his righteousness,
and all these things shall be added unto you."
Matthew 6:33

"Delight yourself also in the LORD,
and He shall give you the desires of your heart."
Psalm37:4

MY HEART AND MY SPIRIT VERSUS THE INDWELLING OF GOD'S SPIRIT

Proverbs 4:23
"Guard your heart with all vigilance, for from it are the sources of life."

MY SPIRIT AND MY "HEART-BRAIN"

All are familiar with the brain sitting in our skull, but little is known of the second independent brain that is located in our heart. Humans have about 100 billion nerves in the brain and only 40,000 nerves in the "heart-brain," which can sense, feel, learn, and remember.

Research has shown that the heart is also a sensory organ that receives and processes information and then sends information back to the brain that stimulates certain activities in the body. **The nervous system of the heart has the ability to learn, build memory, do emotional processing, and even make functional decisions, independent of the brain. The heart also constantly sends information via the nerves to the brain that affects your perception of things.**

The heart generates an electro-magnetic field that is about 5000x stronger than the electro-magnetic field of the brain. This electro-magnetic field is rhythmic according to the heart rate and has a direct influence on the rhythm of the brain. The heart and brain rhythms are in sync with each other.

The heart also works hand in hand with the
- front part of the brain that is also known as the pre-frontal brain/cortex and the
- free will center that obviously has to make the choices.

The "heart-brain" is literally the counselor and "conscience" that recommends the free will center in decision making – e.g., what would be best, to do in a situation and what not. The "heart brain" functions directly as the conscience and is the "little silent voice" that often warns of dangerous thoughts and decisions, and which lovingly encourages us to make and carry out certain positive decisions.

THE HOLY SPIRIT SPEAKS TO OUR SPIRIT THROUGH OUR HEART.

The "heart-brain" gives the free will center the best recommendation regarding a matter. For example, when you have self-centered thoughts that begin in your soul - in your mind's free will center. The final choice must be taken by the free will center, hopefully following the recommendation of the "heart-brain."
Another example:
The "heart brain" advises your mind to accept a specific positive thought and meditate further on it, because it is good and right, full of peace and order and will result in calm.
The free will center has to make the final decision to accept it and if it does, the positive impact is experienced in the soul (emotionally and psychologically) as well as in the body as it leads to the secretion of hormones and chemicals that keep the body in healthy balance and bring about a sense of well-being.

If the thoughts you are having are chaotic, full of fear, aggressive, loaded with anger, hate, unforgiveness, bitterness and negativity, and you choose to accommodate it in your mind and soul, neurotoxic chemicals and hormones are secreted into the body, as well as into the brain cells. These neurotoxic chemicals and hormones flow over the neurons/nerve system in your brain cells, encouraging the formation of a "thornbush" nerve network, which result into

106

continuous negative emotions which are repeatedly activated. This toxic process was <u>initiated</u> by the wrong choice of the free will center.

Thoughts and emotions are basically synonymous with each other. Emotion gives quality and sense to a thought. When negative thoughts with associated negative emotions come into being, they can be so prominent that they numb and dominate the silent voice of the "heart brain," making it difficult to distinguish between right and wrong.

It is often in these types of situations that we experience that our prayers are not being answered or that we cannot hear the voice of the Lord. In fact, it is our own negative toxic thoughts and emotions that get in the way of God's answer.

The spiritual "battlefield" is therefore right at our free will center where the choice must be made to accept or reject thoughts. So, when we decide against the "heart brain's" voice and recommendations, we make a fleshly decision.
For example:
If aggressive, angry, bitter thoughts with the associated negative emotions regarding a particular person would arise in our minds and we would listen to our "heart-brain" voice and reject these thoughts choosing to forgive and release the person instead, your "heart-brain" would secrete a chemical substance/hormone called, **"Atrial Natriuretic Factor" (ANF).**

❖ **ANF is a hormone containing RNA (genetic material carrying a certain message and prescription), which gives it the ability to connect with other RNA according to its built-in prescriptions and is secreted by the heart muscle cells.**
❖ **ANF can bring peace, calm and even happiness to your whole body.**
❖ **ANF therefore has a healing effect on your emotions and body and helps the brain to have clear thinking.**
❖ ANF also exerts control over the water and mineral balance; controls your blood pressure; controls the secretion of other hormones, including sex hormones and even exerts control over the sugar balance in the body.
The WHOLE BODY is therefore in a positive balance – in equilibrium when this chemical/hormone is activated by the "heart brain".

BUT....

If you make your final decision AGAINST the recommendation of your "heart-brain" voice and instead prefer to meditate and dwell on these negative, toxic thoughts, so that bitterness and unforgiveness are engraved in your memory, the "heart-brain" will **NOT secrete the ANF.** This causes **an imbalance to be experienced throughout the BODY and EMOTIONS, resulting in a toxic state, and activating the long-term disease in the body**, in other words, ignoring the "heart-brain" voice, results in the formation of mostly long-term diseases.

Your heart is therefore not just a mechanical pump, but the strongest oscillator – electro-mechanical mechanism in your body that releases a specific unique rhythm into you. This rhythm also determines the rhythm of your brain function. When the heart rhythm via the release of ANF brings peace and calm, you experience a psychological and physical balance that promotes health.
An imbalance in this rhythm means physical imbalance, mental discomfort, and physical illness.

So, the quality of life and health we enjoy depends on the quality of thinking we cherish!
As we submit our thoughts to Jesus according to **2 Corinthians 10:4,5,** and act in line with His Word, the Holy Spirit will help us to make the right decisions and maintain the necessary self-discipline.

Toxic thoughts are predominantly fear-driven and result in the whole body transitioning into a survival-fight-flight response, accordingly, secreting the various hormones. This brings the body into a temporary state of imbalance. If these toxic thoughts persist long-term, they begin to work "self-destructively" on the body.

The main hormone secreted in this regard, which results in a chain reaction of over secretion of other hormones, is <u>Cortisol</u> (secreted by the adrenal glands). This whole process is initiated by the hypothalamus, which is a small but very important gland in the brain, acting like the main power station in the body, and is stimulated by the mental state of your heart and brain.

<u>An example of such a toxic pattern of thinking</u> and its consequences: -
Prolonged stress, anxiety, fear, depression

Prolonged exposure to hormone e.g., Cortisol

Suppression and destruction of immunity cells, e.g., T-cells

Immune related diseases and metabolic dysfunction,
E.g. Chronic fatigue syndrome,
     Chemical Sensitivity/Allergy Syndrome (MCS/EI),
     Low Blood sugar levels,
     Lazy thyroid, etc.
When we allow these toxic thoughts to take root in our brain's cells through our memory banks, we build the wall of sin that the Lord speaks of in **<u>Isaiah 59:1,2:</u>**
"Behold, the hand of the Lord is not too short to save, nor is His ear too heavy to hear; But your iniquities have separated between you and your God, and your sins have hidden His face from you, so that He will not hear."

The Lord wants to help us but waits for us to get our lives back in line with His will.

These sins and toxic thoughts, which we so often cherish, bring
➢   Separation between man and God.
➢   Separation between man and self.
➢   Separation between man and his/her neighbor (other people)
➢   And have a physical and psychological impact on our body.

It is defined in the Bible in various places:
Among other things, James points to the healing effect that repentance (spoken word) has on the body in **James 5;16 "So confess your sins to one another and pray for one another so that you may be healed. The prayer of a righteous person has great effectiveness**."
David writes in Psalm **103:2-3** how the Lord forgives our sins and at the same time heals our diseases: "Praise the LORD, O my soul! Do not forget all His kind deeds! **He is the One who forgives all your sins, who heals all your diseases…**"

Proverbs 17:20 shows us the following:" **The one who has a perverse heart does not find good**, and the one who is deceitful in speech falls into trouble."

In Deuteronomy 10:16 and Jeremiah 4:4, the Lord commands His people to **circumcise their hearts** rather than circumcise the physical. This circumcision of the heart is needed when a **hardened heart developed due to sin** and here, we are recommended to examine ourselves

and lay down the sin that separates us and God. In Romans 2:28-29, we see the following statement Paul makes: "For a person is not a Jew who is one outwardly, nor is circumcision something that is outward in the flesh, but someone is a Jew who is one inwardly, and **circumcision is of the heart by the Spirit and not by the written code. This person's praise is not from people but from God.**"
Colossians 2:11 confirms the above, telling us that there is a heart circumcision that is **not done by hands,** but **by the working of the Spirit of Jesus Christ so that fleshly, sinful practices can be renounced.**

When we align with Abba Father's will in our lives and allow the Holy Spirit to speak into our spirit and heart, we come into the healthy balance of the "heart-brain" and mind as Abba Father created us to be, which can then result in healing.

"Let not your heart be troubled; Believe in God, believe also in Me."
John 14:1.
"Trust in the Lord with all your heart and
do not lean upon your own understanding."
Proverbs 3:5

SEALED WITH THE HOLY SPIRIT

2 Corinthians 1:21,22
"But it is God who establishes us, together with you,
in Christ and who anointed us,
who <u>also sealed us and gave us the Spirit in our hearts</u>,
as a down payment."

2 Corinthians 5:5 also confirms this special quality of the Holy Spirit, namely, that <u>we are sealed with the Holy Spirit</u>, but <u>also receive Him as a pledge</u> (down payment).

HOW CAN WE BE SEALED WITH THE HOLY SPIRIT?

This word brings new meaning to the qualities and character of the Holy Spirit:
"Sealed "meaning:
- ❖ A "trademark" of **Quality**
- ❖ An Outward **Guarantee**
- ❖ A point of **origin and identity** from where it came from

You can probably already see where I'm aiming for, yes, it's really great to think that the indwelling Holy Spirit is almost our "Trademark," adding the 3 above qualities to our lives. When Abba Father looks at us, we are also known to Him over the rest of humanity. For the world, there is also an outward sign that we have "something", which they do not have and that they do need... I think that this is the reason why people often also approach Holy Spirit-filled people when they seek help with their personal problems. Their realization that there is a divine quality to our lives, which can give them security and stability, draws them to us.

WHAT DOES IT MEAN TO HAVE THE HOLY SPIRIT AS A PLEDGE?

"Pledge" in this context means:
- ❖ Guarantee
- ❖ Promise/Agreement
- ❖ Collateral Security

It's more of a personal "guarantee" that the Lord gives us, as His children. A guarantee of **His indwelling presence in our hearts;** A guarantee that we are inseparably connected to Him! The Holy Spirit is the concrete proof of God's promises for us.

Jesus promised that He would send a Comforter and He did. In John 14:16,17,26, the promise of the Holy Spirit is defined by Jesus Himself, and it is a whole "package" that we receive. It is such a powerful sense that God's abundant presence is permanently in our heart!

Today, the Holy Spirit feels as close to me as every breath I take, after all, He also represents the life that has been breathed into us.

Jesus certainly did not leave us orphaned but gave us a wonderful "gift" of closeness so that we would never have to feel God-forsaken.

WHAT ABOUT THE HOLY SPIRIT'S QUALITY OF COLLATERAL SECURITY?

It is so unique to God's character to give in abundance! The Holy Spirit is our security in the midst of an evil world and if we look deeper into the meaning of what collateral means, it makes this security even more special!

COLLATERAL means:
- ❖ side by side.
- ❖ related.
- ❖ supplementary certainty and
- ❖ blood relative in the sideline.

Well, there you have it! Abba Father's Spirit works side by side in and from without us! He is our enduring assurance and security that God is faithful to His promises and that He will manifest Himself in and from us. He has sealed His connection to us with Jesus' blood so that we can be "blood relatives" of Him, joint heirs with Christ! Please read Romans 8:15-17. Isn't that "awesome"? The Lord blesses us so incredibly much that we don't always grasp the full concept of it until He reveals Himself in such small moments as this one.

"For you did not receive the spirit of slavery leading again to fear,
but you received the Spirit of adoption,
by whom we cry, "Abba, Father."
The Spirit Himself bears witness to our spirit
that we are God's children and if children,
then heirs (namely, heirs of God and also
fellow heirs with Christ) – if indeed
we suffer with Him so we may also be glorified with Him."
Romans 8:15-17

Thank you, Jesus, for sending your Spirit
as a pledge and seal to us
Thank you for choosing to be so intimate with us.
by dwelling in our hearts, by your Spirit.
Please make me more aware of Your presence and
Make me more sensitive to Your voice.
Thank you that I am sealed with Your Spirit and
That I may find my strength in You.
In Jesus' Name Alone
Amen.

MY HEART AND THE SEED OF GOD'S KINGDOM

Matthew 13:1-23

Matthew 13:3
"He told them many things in parables,
saying: "Listen!
A Sower went out to sow..."

We see in Matthew 13 how Jesus in parables reveals to the people the Kingdom of heaven's principles. It's a new and almost "strange" message for these law-bound people, yet they follow Jesus to hear more.

The problem with which the hearers/audience, who were mainly Israelites/Jews, Scribes and Pharisees, was that their general perceptions were shaped by the Torah since they had no New Testament as a guide. The New Testament had not yet been written. The people followed the teaching of the Pharisees, the Scribes, and the laws of Moses ' time and served God accordingly. They still had the expectation of the Messiah, but no realization that He had already come! It is in view of this that Jesus says to His disciples in Matthew 13:13-16: "For this reason I speak to them in parables: Although **they see they do not see**, and although **they hear they do not hear, nor do they understand**. And concerning them, the prophecy of Isaiah is fulfilled that says: '**You will listen carefully yet will never understand, you will look closely yet will never comprehend. For the heart of this people has become dull; they are hard of hearing, and they have shut their eyes, so that they would not see with their eyes and hear with their ears and understand with their hearts and turn, and I would heal them.**" "**But your (the disciples') eyes are blessed because they see, and your ears because they hear**. For I tell you the truth, many prophets and righteous people longed to see what you see but did not see it, and to hear what you hear but did not hear it."

In this **context, Jesus Himself is the Sower.** He continues, despite the people not having the true insight they need, as well as their wrong perceptions, to instruct them in the new message of the Kingdom of God and its accompanying principles. They are caught up in the legalistic practices of the Torah and the "preaching" of the church leaders that make them spiritually blind and deaf. Yet there may be some who will hear the true message of the Kingdom, for Jesus says in verse 12 that He who has will be given to him in abundance... Here, Jesus is not speaking about position or possessions, but about insight into the secrets or mysteries of the Kingdom of heaven. Even the disciples did not have this insight, so Jesus also instructs them.

In this chapter, Jesus tells, among other things, three parables, in one of which He compares the Kingdom of heaven to seed. Remember, as defined in previous parts of the book, that seed carries specific DNA/genetic characteristics that are unique to its purpose. This kingdom seed carries the unique doctrine of the Gospel of Jesus Christ that dominates the Old Testament message as it came to an end when Jesus arrived on earth to bring this New Testament into effect with His death and resurrection or to make it valid as such. Please read about this in Hebrews 8:6-8-12, Hebrews 9:14-16-17 and Hebrews 10:9-10. It is very important to understand this fact of the Old and New Testament.

When Jesus explained in Matthew 13:14-15 that the people's hearts had grown dull and they could hardly hear or see, He actually made the point that the purpose of His teaching was according to Isaiah's prophecy, hoping that the people would begin to understand what He wanted to teach them, but their hearts were cold to the Word of the Lord. How do we know this? We see this according to the comparison that Jesus draws between the four conditions of the heart of the people in the parable of the Sower. He wanted them to measure themselves against the different types of hearts so that they could determine where their heart would fit. We need to do the same. How receptive are <u>we</u> to the seed of the Kingdom of heaven?

The whole of Matthew 13 is actually aimed at the church leaders of that time. We see this when Jesus addresses them specifically in Matthew 13:52, saying: "... "Every expert in the law..." Thus, this chapter also deals with the resistance to the teaching of Jesus that the Scribes displayed. Therefore, we see that these teachers and experts of the law who taught of the people were blind leaders without insight and understanding, which would also bring blind followers without insight.

We need to reflect in this regard also on what dogmas of church leaders we listen to and what spiritual seed we allow to take residence in our hearts and germinate and which do not. It is in the light of this, that it is important to examine the Truth of the Word of the Lord under the guidance of the Holy Spirit as well.

THE FOUR CONDITIONS OF THE HEART IN THE PARABLE OF THE SOWER IN MATTHEW 13:

First Heart (verse 19)
Here the kingdom seed fell by the wayside and was picked up by the birds. These people do not understand the message of the Kingdom, so it has no value to them. They do not even think about it anymore but forget it. So, Satan robs them of the eternal truth of the Kingdom.

Second Heart (verse 20)
The kingdom seed falls on rocky places, where plants cannot take deep root here and wither and die in the sun. It is the rocky hearts that are a metaphor of the law written on stone tables. The roots of the Kingdom cannot take root there since the stone heart cannot be penetrated. When this person is persecuted by other legalistic people, they quickly lose the little faith they had.

Third Heart (verse 22)
The thorny heart is full of deceptive dogmas and does not focus at all on the Central Message of the Kingdom of Heaven. Their focus is on self-enrichment and self-exaltation. Jesus is not in the picture at all.

Fourth Heart (verse 23)
This heart's soil is fertile and prepared to receive Kingdom seed. It is this well-prepared heart that understands and responds to the word of the Kingdom of Heaven. The response also includes conduct in line with Kingdom principles. These individuals' lives yield spiritual fruit, 30-, 60- and 100-fold. It is also unselfish fruitage where it is not for his own glory but to honor Jesus.

It is therefore important to listen and understand what the Kingdom of Heaven and the Gospel of Jesus Christ are all about and not remain trapped in the general circular inaccurate dogmatics of modern religions. The Gospel that Jesus Christ preached was a Gospel drenched in love, not condemnation. **Examine the Truth of the Word of the Lord and Live according to It.**

In Hosea we see how the Lord demonstrates through Hosea's life what spiritual obstacles Israel was living with.
In Hosea 14:2, the Lord says to the people: "Repent, ... to the Lord your God, for you have stumbled because **of your iniquity."**
Hosea 12:7 says, "And you must return to your God, **exercise love and justice, and hope in your God continually."**
Jeremiah **4:3 says, "For thus says the Lord: "Break up your fallow land, and do not sow among thorns."**

It is remarkable how these verses relate to what Jesus said in Matthew 13. It's just put in a different context.

In Biblical times, it was the custom of the Sower to first sow his seed by hand and <u>then</u> plow it in. This resulted in some seed being lost, because it did not fall on the good soil, where the Sower would plow.

Considering this practice, God tells the people to first clean the fallow land before sowing. It's a practice they could relate to.

A fallow land is ground that has not been ploughed for a long time.. The soil is hard and there was more than enough opportunity for seeds of weeds to germinate and grow. It would not be wise to want to use such land according to the customs of that time, without even cleaning it.

Yet we see that the Lord wanted to convey a spiritual message that still applies today.

The fallow land lies right inside our hearts. The Israelites were not unfamiliar with God, nor are we. So, this message is not meant for the person who has never met the Lord.

How often does it happen that our busy life or our own laziness draws us away from our First Love, Jesus Christ? We can find 10,000 other things to do rather than spend time with God. In the process, our hearts become a fallow land. Our heart's soil is hard and dry, not suitable for good seed. The weeds of various "sins" and bad habits slowly but surely creep into our hearts and begin to grow until there is no more fertile ground left, in which the Kingdom seed of God, can grow. Often this seed of sin creeps unnoticed into our hearts, and only when it has reached maturity do, we realize we are in trouble. We begin wrestling with rebellion against God and it becomes difficult to lay down these bad things in our lives again. Nor can we serve God halfheartedly, while the thorns of our iniquity "choke" the love, the Word, and righteousness of God.

James 4:4 reminds us that we cannot be friends with the world and with God at the same time, for they stand as enemies before one another. God wants to have a growing love relationship with us. In such a relationship, there is no place for other things that take priority over Him. We need to be silent from time to time before the Lord and look at the condition of our hearts. Is it a fallow land or is it fertile ground in which the good seed of the Lord can grow??

The same recommendation that God gave to Israel years ago, He is giving to us today in Hosea 10:12:

> *"Sow to yourselves in righteousness,*
> *reap in mercy.*
> *break up your fallow ground:*
> *(Meaning that you should prepare the soil of your heart,*
> *Cleaning it and making it ready*
> *To receive Kingdom seed)*
> *for it is time to seek the LORD,*
> *till He comes and rains righteousness upon you.*
> *(Jesus is our righteousness who delivers us from sinful living.)*
> *Hosea 10:12*

THE LORD IS MY SHEPHERD

Psalm 23
Psalm of David.
The LORD is my shepherd.
I shall not want.
He makes me to lie down in green pastures:
He leads me beside the still waters.
He restores my soul:
He leads me in the paths of righteousness
for His Name's sake.
Yea, though I walk through the valley of the shadow of death,
I will fear no evil: for You are with me,
Your rod and Your staff they comfort me.
You prepare a table before me
in the presence of my enemies:
You anoint my head with oil,
my cup runs over.
Surely goodness and mercy shall follow me
all the days of my life: and
I will dwell in the house of the LORD forever.

As David speaks to his Heavenly Father, he discloses his experience with Him as his Shepherd. He relates the characteristics of a shepherd to God with a spiritual context, revealing to us how wonderful and caring God is towards His people, revealing a deeper meaning to us. This Psalm can also be used as a form of prayer and worship as we glorify God as our wonderful Shepherd who cares for us.

The Lord is my Shepherd...
Thank you, Father, for being my Shepherd, for moving ahead of me on my path of life, making my path straight, changing every stumbling block into steppingstones toward spiritual growth.

I shall not want.
Just think for a moment how God provides for your needs in your life. In another Psalm David writes that the righteous will not go hungry but will be provided for. Jesus says that our Heavenly Father provides for our basic needs just as He provides for the sparrow and the lilies of the field. Read about this in Mathew 6:25-31.

He makes me to lie down in green pastures...
Our Lord and Shepherd does not only provide for our physical needs but also for our spiritual hunger. His Word brings peace and rest for us as we put our trust in Him. Jesus proclaims in the New Testament that He is the Bread of Life. See John 6:8.

He leads me beside the still waters.
The water that Jesus gives us, is the Spirit filled Word of Truth which quenches our spiritual thirst bringing calm and peace to our spirit and soul. Jesus is truly our Prince of Peace.

He restores my soul...
The healing power of His Spirit is at our disposal— we must just give the Lord a chance to heal our broken spirit and soul, so that His refreshing power can flow through our whole being and do a perfect work.

He leads me in the paths of righteousness for His Name sake.
The Lord takes us on the path of forgiveness and mercy. When we accept His forgiveness and grace and also forgive others, He puts His cloak of righteousness around our shoulders, the garment that carries the redemptive power of Jesus. In the process, then, we come into the right relationship with Him who sits on the throne and can boldly approach the throne of God with our requests and heart's prayers...

Yea, though I walk through the valley of the shadow of death,
Even in the midst of life-threatening circumstances, difficult circumstances, and problems for which we do not have answers and in the midst of depression, our Shepherd stands ready to lead us out of there and take us to the mountaintops of spiritual victory. Where I am too weak, He carries me. Where our powers cease, His eternal, miracle-working power takes over, so I will not be afraid.

Your rod and Your staff they comfort me.
The Lord's protection is always at our disposal. Should we blindly choose the wrong path, it will be the Shepherd's staff that draws us back to Him. If we were trapped somewhere on a rock, because of our own wrong choices or being ensnared in a forest of sin, it is His staff that guides us out and brings us to His side to safety. His staff, His Word will guide us, if we are willing to listen and obey.

You prepare a table before me in the presence of my enemies...
And when people want to harm us, to bring us down, when Satan attempts to attack us, the Lord offers His eternal protection and reveals His powerful workings to the enemy. He plainly declares that He protects His flock and surrounds it with prosperity. Why? Because we are His lawful property, and He will not allow the enemy to destroy us.

You anoint my head with oil; my cup runs over.
Oil was used in Biblical times by the shepherds to bring healing to the wounds that a sheep may have. It also kept the insects away that may cause festering of the wounds. Please read Psalm147:3 about this.. Oil also refers to the anointing of the Holy Spirit. It is true that when the Holy Spirit drenches our lives and is in control of our thinking and whole being, then our heart's cup will overflow with praise for our Abba Father, our Shepherd. Rightly, Jesus said in John that streams of living waters will flow from within us and that is exactly what happens when we give the Holy Spirit free control in our lives and allow Him to reveal and interpret His Word to us. Also read John 7:37-39.

Surely goodness and mercy shall follow me all the days of my life...
An active, growing relationship with our God and Shepherd, where we walk continually in His presence, brings abundant goodness and favor to our lives, for His blessings are part of His promises to us. This is also confirmed by the Psalm writer in Psalm 37:4: "Delight thyself also in the LORD; and He shall give you the desires of your heart."

And I will dwell in the house of the LORD forever.
The result is eternal life in the direct presence of our Lord and Savior and Shepherd.

Amen

"Jesus says, "I am the good Shepherd, and
I know My own and am known by My own.
Just as the Father knows Me, so I know the Father.
And I lay down My life for the sheep.
My sheep listen to My voice, and
I know them, and they follow Me.
And I give them eternal life, and
They will never be lost, and
No one will snatch them out of My hand.
My father, who gave them to Me, is greater than all.
and no one can snatch them out of My Father's hand.
My father and I are one."
John 10:15–16, 27–30

WHEN JESUS BECOMES MY GREATEST JOY AND DELIGHT...

Psalm 37:4,5
" Then you will take delight in the LORD,
and He will answer your prayers.
Commit your future to the LORD!
Trust in Him, and He will act on your behalf."

"For **with You is the fountain of life: in Your light shall we see light.**
O continue Your lovingkindness unto **them that know You;** and **Your righteousness to the upright in heart.**' Psalm 36:9-10.

The Word of the Lord is refreshing and new every day, just as it is to be continually in His presence! The question is, are you living in His presence, is He your highest joy and delight??

David clearly knew the secret of how-to live-in God's enduring presence and left us the keys to open this secret in our lives: -
Re-read Psalm 37:4,5, also in the old translation, so that you can appreciate the full value of these verses.

DAVID'S RECOMMENDATIONS CAN BE DEFINED AS FOLLOWS: -

- ❖ Focus on the Lord. Let Him always be the center of your existence.
- ❖ Make **Him your greatest joy and delight** in your life. It's a real choice you must make.
- ❖ Trust in the Lord with heart and soul.
- ❖ Allow the Lord to be a priority in your life. In this way, He will take care of you.
- ❖ A halfhearted surrender cannot put you within God's abundant blessing, for Satan still has opportunity to rob you of your blessings. God wants to take care of you in total and that's why He demands a 100% surrender! Part of God's care is His protection for you, but it's only possible if all the spiritual doors in your life are closed.
- ❖ The more time I spend in God's presence, through prayer, two-way communication with Him, reading His Word, and seeking the fellowship of other sincere children of the Lord, the greater God becomes a reality in my life, the more I get to know His character, which will result in this very joy in the Lord. See Psalm 36:10,11.

WHAT ARE THE CONSEQUENCES OF THIS WAY OF LIFE IN THE LORD?

- ❖ **God gives us the desires of** our hearts. The Lord often understands our heart's desire better than we understand it ourselves and fulfills it in such a wonderful, surprising way that one is amazed.
- ❖ Precisely because the Lord knows and understands us in depth, our desires and needs can be perfectly fulfilled by Him.
- ❖ We are wrapped up in God's caring love. It is His eternal love that brings back beauty into a broken world and brings healing to hearts, when needed.
- ❖ Psalm 36:8-10 makes us aware of the abundance we experience in the Lord when we live in surrender to Him. We enjoy the abundance that only God can give as described in the following verses: " They shall be abundantly satisfied with the fatness of Your house; and You shall make them drink of the river of Your pleasures. For with You is the fountain of life: in Your light shall we see light. O, continue Your lovingkindness unto them that know You; and Your righteousness to the upright in heart."

LIVING IN GOD'S PRESENCE MEANS LIVING IN ABUNDANCE

What does this abundance entail?
It includes spiritual abundance as well as material and emotional abundance, for God cares for us in totality and wants us to experience abundance and fulfillment in EVERY facet of our life.

Along with this abundance comes the heavenly bread with which He feeds us and the bubbling living fountain-waters of His Holy Spirit with which He refreshes our soul and satisfies our spiritual hunger and thirst. It's a feast! His bounty! Read John 10:10.

What makes this abundance so outstanding, is that it brings us to the point of new meaning to life — that which makes life worthwhile. In Him we experience what life really is; In God lies what man so intensely craves. What is often not realized, is that this yearning can be satisfied precisely **in God's presence!**

Psalm 37:4 says: **"Delight yourself also in the LORD; and He shall give you the desires of your heart."** (New KJV)
Delighting yourself in the Lord, means to enjoy His constant presence, having quality time with Him and getting to know His will, through His Word in the Bible. In the process your love for Him grows stronger and you naturally start to live more according to His Kingdom principles. This way of living, results in your desires coming into alignment with His will. So, when you pray for the fulfilment of your desires, you will receive it because it is in line with God's will.

Why not make a determined choice today to make the Lord your greatest joy, regardless of the circumstances? God's Word stands firm and what He promises He performs, so He will also give you the desires of your heart.

Abba Father, I am making a new decision today
to surrender,
To put You first in my life,
to make You my greatest joy and delight.
I know that out of my own, I am not strong enough
to do it all the time,
Therefore, I ask that You please
strengthen me by Your Holy Spirit.
I don't want to serve You
just for what I receive out of Your hand,
but desire to be continually in Your presence,
for in You alone I am happy and fulfilled.
Thank you for all the blessings I receive from Your hand.
Let my life be a joy to You.
In Jesus' Name Alone
Amen

IV. HOW GREAT IS OUR GOD!

"This is what the LORD says:
"The heavens are My throne
and the earth is My footstool."

"Who has measured out the waters in the hollow of his hand,
or carefully measured the sky,
or carefully weighed the soil of the earth,
or weighed the mountains in a balance,
or the hills on scales?
Who comprehends the mind of the LORD,
or gives Him instruction as His counselor?
To whom can you compare God?
To what image can you liken Him
He is the One who sits on the earth's horizon;
its inhabitants are like grasshoppers before Him.
He is the one who stretches out the sky like a thin curtain,
and spreads it out like a pitched tent
Do you not know? Have you not heard?
The LORD is an eternal God,
the Creator of the whole earth.
He does not get tired or weary;
there is no limit to His wisdom."
Isaiah 66:1a & Isaiah 40:12,13,18,22,28

"JEHOVAH SHAMMAH"

Hosea 14:6
"I will be to Israel like the dew," says the Lord.

God's omnipresence was almost tangible with the early morning misty clouds all around us, this morning. As the misty clouds faded away and the sunrays burst through the clouds, the crystal-clear dewdrops sparkled like diamonds making the sense of God's presence so much stronger.

When I think of His Spirit, who also has made my spirit and body His dwelling place, I see in my mind's eye His dynamic working in people's lives and so also in my own. Then there are times like now, when one becomes more aware of His gentle, loving, peaceful, refreshing presence, such as the omnipresent misty clouds all around us, when He comes to calm our restless spirit, in that He turns the constant anxieties into divine peace, and wraps His love around our heart like a warm blanket...

His presence is refreshing, and new every morning, like the dewdrops on the leaves. It reminds me anew of David's words, "He restores my soul..." Yes, it is true, Abba Father's omnipresence restores the troubled soul and revives it anew in His power. Just as the plants of this earth depend on the dew and rain for survival, we depend on God's refreshing divine influence in our spirit and soul. Without it, we will wither and languish like a bush in the desert.

For the Israelites, the dew was also part of God's blessing, abundance, and prosperity. When it would dry up and no longer be there, after the night had passed, it would be a sign of the need of self-examination. They needed to ask themselves: Did they turn their backs on the Lord that the Lord was also withholding His blessings?

In Numbers 11:9 we see how the dew in the desert was associated with part of God's provision and caring for Israel: "And when **the dew came down on the camp in the night, the manna fell with it.** God did not only provide the physical "bread" in the form of manna but **initiated the awareness of Him in a spiritual sense**. Their outcry for food was answered but **they needed to learn that they need to set aside quality time for prayer and worship so that their spiritual life could also be nourished by God's Spirit. In the same way we need to set aside time in which our spirit could be nourished by God's Spirit.**

In Deuteronomy 32, Moses sings a song at the Lord's command. Here we see in verse 2 how "dew" is used symbolically to the spoken word. Verse 2 says: "**My doctrine shall drop as the rain, my speech shall distil as the dew, as the small rain upon the tender herb, and as the showers upon the grass.**" Surely this teaching would come from the Lord and be ministered with grace and love to people.

Jesus also invites us in John 7:37 with these words: "... **If anyone thirsts, let him come to Me and drink. He that believes in Me, as the Scripture says, "Streams of living water shall flow out of his belly."** Jesus' Spirit-inspired Word will refresh, build us up, restore and cause us to "overflow" to His glory.

Make time to stand still in the refreshing presence of God, so that He can revive your spirit and soul anew by pouring out within you the freshness of His Spirit. Allow Him to be "JEHOVA SHAMMAH" – meaning "God is present", "God is here", for you. It is in these moments that you will grow spiritually and get to know His voice more clearly.

In His enduring presence in your life, also within you, where He came to make His dwelling place, you will find strength for each day, and you will hear His voice when He speaks to you through His Word.

So let us acknowledge Him!
Let us seek to acknowledge the LORD!
<u>He will come to our rescue</u> as certainly as the appearance of the dawn,
as certainly as the winter rain comes,
as certainly as the spring rain that waters the land."

Hosea 6:3

SEARCHING FOR GOD'S GLORY

Exodus 33:18-23
"And Moses said, "Show me Your glory."
And the LORD said, "I will make all my goodness pass before your face,
and I will proclaim the LORD by name before you.
I will be gracious to whom I will be gracious,
I will show mercy to whom I will show mercy."
But He added, "You cannot see my face,
for no one can see Me and live."
The LORD said, "Here is a place by Me,
you will station yourself on a rock.
When My glory passes by, I will put you in a cleft in the rock
and will cover you with My hand while I pass by.
Then I will take away My hand, and you will see My back,
but My face must not be seen."

We read of several people in the Bible who experienced the glory of God in various ways. Not all the people had the privilege of seeing or experiencing God in special ways.

One such person, of which we read very little in the Bible, is Enoch. In Genesis 5:24 and Hebrews 11:5, we read that Enoch walked with God and that he pleased God in such a way that God took him up into heaven without him dying. What was so unique about his life with God? He was able to experience the glory of God arising from a very intimate relationship with God.

Noah also had a unique relationship with God. God chose him above all others to perform for Him a task that has never been accomplished on this earth until that time. He asks Noah to build an ark so that God can save his family, while God's judgment is poured out in the form of a floodwater over the entire earth! Noah's faith must have been of outstanding quality, to be able to push through with such an almost impossible task! What made Noah's faith so outstanding was also the fact that up to that time nothing like rain had fallen from heaven. For a hundred-and twenty-years Noah and his sons had been building this God-given boat under the flood of mockery of the wicked people who lived around them. I can't help wondering how we would react to such a mission! Would we have been able persevere for 120 years and remain steadfast in our faith? We read in Genesis 6:8,9 what attractive qualities Noah had in the Lord's eyes: "But **Noah found favor in the sight of the Lord**. ... Noah was a **righteous, upright man among his contemporaries. He walked with God.**"

From Genesis 11 to chapter 22, we read of another special man who caught God's attention. This man is Abraham. God reveals His glory through conversations, dreams, visions, and visits from heavenly guests (angels). God went even further and made a covenant with Abraham that He had passed to the letter. What made God willing to go an "extra mile" with Abraham? Abraham had an unwavering faith in God and expected the humanly impossible of God and received it after about 25 years. He blindly obeyed by moving away from his homeland as God commanded him to do. God guides him to a new destination he did not know at first. In another incident, Abraham believed that God would raise up his son again and assure his offspring, even if he would let him die as a sacrifice. Read about this in Hebrews 11:8,17,18. Finally, but not least, God showed Abraham the heavenly city! See Hebrews 11:10. What an indescribable privilege! God knew the end from the beginning, so He was able to declare hundreds and thousands of years of events in advance to Abraham. He tells Abraham exactly what would happen to his offspring, long before Isaac was born. Read about it in Genesis 15:13-15.

After Abraham, we see how God reveals His glory in similar ways to Isaac and his wife Rebekah, as well as to Jacob and his wife Rachel and their son, Joseph.

Hundreds of years later, there is a man named Moses chosen by God to lead His people out of Egypt. This man also caught God's attention. He meets him at the burning bush and reveals Himself as the great "I AM WHO I AM" in Exodus 3:14. Moses' relationship with God is so steadfast and intimate that the Bible describes it as a uniquely divine friendship between God and man in Exodus 33:11. God reveals Himself to Moses through direct conversations between Him and Moses, through visits on the mount Sinai, through heavenly visions and through conversations in the Tabernacle that God had set up through Moses, after He had given Moses a heavenly vision and passed on the exact dimensions and precepts to Moses. Read about it in Exodus 25:9.

Moses was an intercessor for the people of Israel. He was unwavering in his faith and obedience to God. He shows his 100% surrender and dependence on God by leading the people many times through life-threatening circumstances, with God's power.

Moses does not hesitate to ask even amid God's discontent with the people, Israel, **"Lord, show me Your glory."** God blesses His friend by showing him His glory, hiding him in the cleft of a rock. What an indescribably wonderful experience this must have been! Read about it in Exodus 33:17-23.

Yet there are times when man shy away from God and His revealed glory. What makes us do this? We see that Israel did not have a chance to move into God's revealed glory. Filled with fear, they preferred that Moses share the messages of God with them. Read about it in Exodus 24:16-18 & Exodus 34:29-35. They also shied away from God's glorious presence because sin was still so prominent in their lives.

Romans 3:23 tells us that **"All have sinned and fall short from the glory of God." Before the fall into sin, Adam and Eve were dressed in God's glory, since they were without sin.** They were able to enjoy God's glorious presence until the day they gave in to the temptation of Satan. **God's glory and presence are not compatible with sin,** so Adam and Eve found themselves to be naked, after the fall event. They now also experience fear and hide from the Lord in the garden. This fear was the result of sin. **God clothes them in animal skins, having offered the first sin offering.** Read about it in Genesis 3:7-11, 21-23 & Genesis 4:4. **Without blood there could never be reconciliation between God and man again, man would never again be able to see and experience the glory of God in such intensity.**

Sin brings separation between God and man, but God's loving outreach to man is not stopped by this. He brings forth out of love and grace, the final Sacrifice that puts man in the power to move into His presence and revealed glory, namely, His Son, Jesus Christ. Please read Hebrews 9:11,12-15a,22-28. What a wonderful privilege we have, to serve such a perfect, loving God!

Have you experienced the revealed glory of God in your life?

In this modern age, the people want to build a 3rd temple so that God's glory can once again descend into it as in the Old Testament, when His glory was found in the Most Holy of the Tabernacle and Temple. Their perspective has not changed over the years around the experiences of the Old Testament to the New Testament lifestyle that Jesus preached and revealed to mankind of which we are a part.

In the **Old Testament**, the people saw an "outward display"/ manifestation of God's glory and His presence. This "outward display" of God's presence and glory brought the people to that place of worship where they saw and experienced the glory of the Lord and His presence. The reason for this was that God did not live in man through His Spirit, but descended on them only at times. One such example is seen in Numbers 11:24-26 where the seventy men of Israel prophesied when the Spirit of the Lord "rested **upon** them." After this incident, we do not see the Spirit of God remaining in them.

In the **New Testament,** we see how this situation has changed. In Matthew 6:5-6, Jesus advises us to go into our secret closet in isolation to practice our worship. He also often climbed a mountain to go and pray in isolation and spend time with God the Father. Such incidents are found in Mark 1:35 and Matthew 14:23, among others.

Jesus promises His disciples who later began to act as Apostles, that when He leaves, as He is going back to His Father, He will send His Spirit to them. In Acts 2:1-7 we see them being **filled with the Holy Spirit.** After this incident, we see the Apostles baptizing the converted people with water in the Name of Jesus Christ and laying hands on them **to receive the Holy Spirit's indwelling into their lives.**

Paul later explains how the glory of the Lord can be restored to our lives.
This restoration process **begins with the process of repentance and rebirth followed with sanctification** through which we are **progressively renewed in spirit and soul**. Our body will follow as spirit and soul "dictate."
As outlined in this book before, Paul explains that Abba Father came to make His dwelling place **in us by His Spirit**, since **we became the temples of the Lord**. We read again
2 Corinthians 6:16-18 which says: "And what mutual agreement does the temple of God have with idols? **For we are the temple of the living God,** just as God said, "**I will live in them and will walk among them, and I will be their God, and they will be my people.**" Therefore "**come out from their midst, and be separate**," says the Lord, "**and touch no unclean thing,** and I will welcome you and **I will be a Father to you, and you will be my sons and daughters," says the All-Powerful Lord.**"
 In other words, if the Spirit of Abba Father came to our habitation, **He also moved in with His glory** as in the Old Testament in the tabernacle and temple.

We see that according to Genesis 3:1-7-10 and Romans 3:23 that mankind became naked after the fall into sin, meaning that the glory of the Lord and His Spirit withdrew from them.
So, part of the question for today is, **how do we get this spiritual robe of glory back?**
Romans 13:14 says: "Instead, put on the Lord Jesus Christ (clothe yourself with Jesus Christ), and make no provision for the flesh to arouse its desires. "Here we find the spiritual key, which is to **clothe ourselves with the character of Jesus Christ**. We need to make the character of Jesus our own and live accordingly. Paul further defines this spiritual garment in Colossians3:9-10,12-17 which says: "Do not lie to one another, since you have put off the old man with its practices and have been clothed with the new man that is being renewed in knowledge according to the image of the one who created it. Therefore, as the elect of God, holy and dearly loved, clothe yourselves with a heart of mercy, kindness, humility, gentleness, and patience, bearing with one another and forgiving one another, if someone happens to have a complaint against anyone else. Just as the Lord has forgiven you, so you also forgive others. And to all these virtues add love, which is the perfect bond. Let the peace of Christ be in control in your heart (for you were in fact called as one body to this peace) and be thankful. Let the word of Christ dwell in you richly, teaching and exhorting one another with all wisdom, singing psalms, hymns, and spiritual songs, all with grace in your hearts to God. And whatever you do in word or deed, do it all in the Name of the Lord Jesus, giving thanks to God the Father through Him." In this passage, Paul describes the characteristics of Jesus that must also be present in our

lives by practicing them for the Lord's glory. In verse 10, Paul refers to the **"new man"** who is **according to the Image of the Creator. It is related to our appearance as before the fall.**

It is the blood of Jesus that cleanses us from all sins and puts us in a position to be able to be before Abba Father without sin. In Revelation 7:14, it speaks of those who have **washed their clothes in the blood of the Lamb:** "... And he said unto me, these are they which come out of the great tribulation, and have **washed their garments, and made them white in the blood of the Lamb."** These believers were clothed in white robes precisely because of what they did. In Revelation 19:8, we see that these **spiritual white robes represent righteous deeds:** "And to her (the bride (the Ecclesia church) was given to be clothed with pure and shining fine linen,** for the fine linen is the righteous deeds of the saints."

In Revelation 16:15 we are warned with these words: "Behold, I am coming as a thief. Blessed is he that **watches, and keeps his garments, lest he walk naked, and they see his shame."** This spiritual white fine linen robe is thus synonymous with the glory of the Lord with which we must be clothed, since it also represents our righteous deeds. In Matthew 22:1-14, Jesus tells a parable of a wedding planned by a king for his son. Everything was ready and when the servants were sent out to invite the guests, there was only trouble. No invited guest wanted to come! On the contrary, they even killed some of the servants on one occasion! Again, the king sent out servants to invite people in the streets to attend the wedding. In verse 11 we see how there was one requirement for these people, they were to have a wedding garment on! When the king found someone who did **not** have a wedding garment, he was removed from this wedding feast. There is clear similarity between this parable and events described in Revelation 19:7-9,10b dealing with the marriage of the Lamb in heaven. There is much symbolism and detail that this passage holds, but for the sake of the subject we are dealing with, I want to mention that **the wedding garment is precisely the white robe of righteous deeds that reflects the glory of the Lord. We see that this king of Matthew 22 was able to distinguish the genuine robe from the robe of deception based on the spiritual garment worn.** Therefore, those who did **not** wear a wedding garment were removed from the wedding feast.

In Revelation 2:1-7, Jesus addresses the congregation of Ephesus about their wrong practices and exhorts them to repent back to Him and His will. If they didn't, Jesus would remove their candlestick, the menorah from them. Here a very serious matter is portrayed. The candlestick/menorah refers partially to the Old Testament seven-point chandelier that was in the Holy of the Tabernacle and Temple that burnt continuously. The symbolism of the light of this candlestick/menorah was the presence of the Holy Spirit. **Here Jesus uses this symbolism to portray the presence of the Holy Spirit in every Ecclesia believer's life. If this congregation did not turn away from their sinful practices, the Holy Spirit would withdraw from them.** What a terrifying thought and condition to be in, should it happen! Just as Jesus warned the congregation, so we are warned today. The presence of the Holy Spirit in us is also representative of the glory of the Lord in us. Here we see similar events to what happened to Adam and Eve when God's glory withdrew from them.

Don't let this warning pass you by but be sensitive to the Word of God's Spirit. Do not be found asleep, as the 5 virgins in Matthew 25:1-13 when the heavenly wedding begins but be watchful and ready. Let the light and glory of God's Spirit be burning continually in your life.

Jesus said:" The person who has My commandments and obeys them
is the one who loves Me.
The one who loves Me will be loved by my Father,
and I will love him and will reveal Myself to him."
John 14:21

Sharon E. De Jager

*Jesus replied, "If anyone loves Me, he will obey My word, and
My Father will love him,
and We will come to him and take up residence with him.
John 14:23*

*Loving Father
I can't help but raise my hands and offer my heart as a
sacrifice before you! You are my God, there is no other like
You. You refresh my soul and make me drink of the living
waters of your Spirit.*

*You are my King, my everything, the fulfillment of my
dreams, the fulfillment of what I yearn for, yes, You are the
Eternal Love that heals hearts, who quenches my spiritual
thirst and feeds my hungry soul... What makes heart's
truths reality and what makes everything so profound!*

*You are holy, O Lord, blessed for ever and ever. Wonderful,
mighty, and powerful.
Jesus, You are my Prince of Peace, my Counselor in difficult
times,
a Mighty God, my "I AM" when the storm rages and
threatens to overwhelm me.
You are my hiding place; You are my Provider, You are my
Comforter, and You are the Center of all my life. Without
Your refreshing presence, I am nothing, just an empty shell.
My Eternal King and Savior! Hallelujah!*

*Abba Father, Jesus, I love you and just want to thank you
for being so wonderful and kind to me. Thank you for the
riches of Your presence. You are God and there is no one
like you.*

*In Jesus' holy name.
Amen*

127

HOPE WITH ETERNAL VALUE

Romans 5:1-5

"Therefore, since we have been <u>declared righteous by faith</u>,
we have peace with God through our Lord Jesus Christ
through whom we have also <u>obtained access by faith</u>
<u>into this grace</u> in which we stand,
and we <u>rejoice in the hope of God's glory</u>
Not only this, but we also rejoice in sufferings,
knowing that <u>suffering produces endurance</u>,
and <u>endurance, character</u>, and <u>character, hope</u>.
<u>And hope does not disappoint</u>,
because the <u>love of God has been poured out in our hearts</u>
through the Holy Spirit who was given to us."

When we look at the struggling world around us, while we ourselves are also under stress because of all the depressing circumstances and challenges, it is very easy to lose our faith and hope in our Almighty Heavenly Father and fall into a pit of hopelessness and depression. Without faith and hope, we cannot move beyond all the heartache, pain, darkness, sickness, and endless physical and psychological struggles. We get into an inability to help ourselves and even others.

In this state of despair, we forget the fact that our hope and power are anchored directly in the Lord Himself and that this Hope and Trust in Him is our Source of life, power, and strength. The Lord makes every day new and gives us a day's portion of His grace, like manna from heaven, to carry us through the day. That's why we can hold on to what the Lord said to Paul in 2 Corinthians 12:9-10: And He said: **"My grace is enough for you, for My power is made perfect in weakness."** So then, I will boast most gladly about my weaknesses, **so that the power of Christ may reside in me**. Therefore, I am **content with weaknesses**, with insults, with troubles, with persecutions and difficulties **for the sake of Christ, for whenever I am weak, then I am strong."**

The moment we turn to Jesus, acknowledge Him as our Savior and Deliverer, and declare our total dependency upon Him, while we seek His face and come into an intimate relationship with Him once again, we will experience a restoration within our spirit, heart, and soul.

Isaiah 30:15 & 18 proclaims the following as God is calling Israel, His chosen people back to Him: "For this is what the Master, the LORD, the Holy One of Israel says:
"If you repented and patiently waited for Me, you would be delivered; if you calmly trusted in Me you would find strength, but you are unwilling.
For this reason **the Lord is ready (waiting impatiently) to show you mercy, He sits on His throne, ready to have compassion on you. Indeed, the Lord is a just God; all who wait for Him in faith will be blessed."**

The same invitation is still extended to us today, namely, to return to God so that He can show us His grace. The Lord waits with impatience for the opportunity to bless us again when we get back in relationship with Him.

As we face the trials, hardships, and challenges of life, the world desperately cries out for any kind of solution and hope they can hold on to, nearly as hanging onto blades of grass hanging

128

over a mountain cliff where they threaten to fall off. **Because of the laxity of most people to examine the truth of God's Word, the Bible, they are ignorant of where to find that hope with eternal value.** They grab onto any temporary something or someone offering hope — the hope that can give them a prosperous, "pandemic-free", future so that they can just get on with their normal wicked existence. Sad but unfortunately true.

The question is......

WHERE DO WE FIND SUCH A SUSTAINABLE HOPE TO CARRY US THROUGH THESE TIMES?
We find it at a point of change of vision, making a definite decision to fix our eyes upon Jesus and NOT on the world of struggles and tribulations.
When our vision is fixed on Jesus Christ and not on worldly circumstances, or our own personal circumstances and challenges, we will start to find new Hope.

David wrote in Psalms 141:8 "**My eyes are continually towards You...**"
Looking with your eyes continually has the same meaning as" looking attentively or gazing upon or to focus upon..." **It points to a specific attentiveness on a specific vision**, e.g. You see the image on the screen of your phone. You are looking attentively at the image while you are receiving information in your mind through your eyes. Your other senses are also attentive as you listen and hear the message. Your eyes and ears enable you to identify and also hear what is said. The two senses are associated with each other while gathering information that will somehow influence your life.

If I should continually focus on the Lord Jesus and NOT turn my eyes towards my problems, challenges, other people or even money, continuously, I will find myself gazing upon the presence of the Lord and hearing His voice through His spoken Word amid my circumstances and challenging situation. His image is being engraved in my mind, inside of me. Therefore, your life is inside your vision, where you are looking most of the time. Read Luke 11:34. So, when you gaze upon the Lord, you receive Him in His fullness and His Light will be within you.

By doing this, you will develop a bigger awareness of your position in Jesus Christ, which will empower you to live from this point. **That on which you focus, will become part of your own personal conduct in life.**

The hope with which we will then deal with life and circumstances will be generated from the living light of Jesus Christ in us. This will result in not living in spiritual and psychological darkness of depression. Read what Jesus says about this in Luke 11:34 and John 8:12. In **John 8:12, Jesus Himself declares that He is the Light of the world and whoever follows Him will NOT walk in darkness but will have the light of life.**

Many people do not have the true life and light of Jesus Christ in their lives because they focus their vision and hope on something or someone else that is NOT life-giving. Nothing else accept Jesus can give us true life.

When you set time aside to give attention to His presence and His voice, you become deeply aware of His presence residing inside of you and the contents of His spoken Word in His voice. This enables you to grow your hope, trust and faith in His character and abilities; getting to know Him more and doing His will which results into blessing.

Our constant focus and vision on Jesus progressively change our conduct in life and generates sustaining life in us that enables us to live in hope and faith.

How do I know that I have lost my attentiveness/my focus on the Lord?
- ➤ When there is a lack of true life due to a lack of love, joy, patience, kindness, faithfulness, gentleness, and self-control, as described in Galatians 5:22,
- ➤ When we find that our state of mind has fallen back into depression and despair.

I then should say:" Lord, I put my attention, my gaze back upon You, Lord.
I turn my eyes, my heart and mind back to gaze upon Your presence."

Hebrews 12:2 reminds us to "keep our eyes on Jesus, who leads us and makes our faith complete..."

We can then actively choose to restore our focus to Jesus and in His power, we will again progressively recover spiritually, psychologically, and emotionally.

"The LORD is my portion, saith my soul,
therefore, will I hope in Him.
The LORD is good unto them that wait for Him,
to the soul that seeks Him.
It is good that a man should both hope and
quietly wait for the salvation of the LORD.
Lamentations 3:24-26

THE RED ROPE OF TRUE HOPE FOR THE NATIONS

Romans 15:12-13
"And again Isaiah says, "The root of Jesse will come,
and the One who rises to rule over the Gentiles (all the nations),
in Him will the Gentiles (all the nations) hope."
Now may the God of hope fill you
with all joy and peace as you believe in Him,
so that you may abound in hope by the power of the Holy Spirit."

Many nations run after all sorts of temporary forms of hope that have no lasting value. In their refusal **to acknowledge God as the only Hope**, the despair in the world grows greater. People have fallen into ignorance of the truth concerning the Lord and have also fallen into hopelessness and deception that make their condition worse.

We read in Revelation of this deception and how the nations are following it, just to worsen their situation without realizing that it is due to their ignorance concerning the Truth that is to be found in Jesus Christ, our Lord. The deception is so severe that it is described as **sorcery**. Interestingly, enough, the word "sorcery" is defined in the Greek as **"pharmakeia"** (G5331). This prophetic word in Revelation 18 and especially verse 23b makes one think deeply about the time in which we are living now. **The nations were deceived because they did not turn to the Lord as their hope.**

Hope is mentioned more than fifty times in the New Testament alone. This makes it an important thing to take note of.

THE ORIGINAL BIBLICAL MEANING OF HOPE...
As you already know, by this time, the New Testament is written in the Greek language and the Old Testament in Hebrew language. To know the true meaning of hope, we need to look at the original words used in the verses and in context of the Bible.

In Romans 15:12-13 we see how the two languages meet it each other in a prophecy of Isaiah as Paul elaborates on hope referring to the Old Testament and bringing it into the presence of the New Testament at that moment. We also see how the prophecy regarding Jesus ' coming was already announced in Isaiah and repeated in Romans by Paul after the prophecy had already been fulfilled with Jesus ' coming to earth. The miracle of this accurate prophecy of Isaiah is that it was prophesied between the years 700 and 690 before Christ's coming to earth. Isaiah is also known as the Messianic Prophet.

Romans 15:12-13 reads as follows: "And again Isaiah says, **"The root of Jesse will come, and the One who rises to rule over the Gentiles (**all the nations), **in Him will the Gentiles (**all the nations**) hope.**" Now may the **God of hope** fill you with all joy and peace as you believe in Him, so that you may abound in **hope** by the power of the Holy Spirit."

In verse 12 which was originally written in the Hebrew language we will find that the word **"hope" = "tikvah"** and in verse 13 we are seeing that "hope" is uttered originally in the Greek language as **"elpis = el-pece"**. The secret is in looking deeper into the meaning of these words which enriches the true meanings of the verses.
Paul connects hope to God as part of His character when he says "...**the God of Hope**"

Elpis/ el-pece (G1680) comes from a root word **"elpo"** meaning **to anticipate, usually with pleasure; expectation (abstract or concrete) or confidence: - faith, hope; expecting and waiting with absolute certainty.**

Paul declares that our **Source of Hope is Jesus Christ, God Himself, giving us hope by the power of His Spirit! This hope gives us stability because of its certainty rooted in Christ Jesus.**

There are many different Hebrew words for "hope" in the <u>Old Testament</u>. They are linked together in their meaning and linked to trust.
Examples in the Old Testament are as follows: -

- Psalm 39:7 Hope = "tocheleth/to-kheh-leth" (H8431) meaning "expectation"
- Psalm 42:5 Hope = "yachal" (H3176) meaning "to wait, to be patient, to hope and trust"
- **Psalm 71:5 & Jeremiah 29:11 Hope = "tikvah/tikvaw" (H8615) meaning "expectancy/ expectation, <u>a rope/chord (to save from the enemy)</u>, comes from a root word meaning to bind or to wait for, or wait upon**

In Romans 15:12 we see that Jesus is described as the Hope for all nations, for the Gentiles and Israel, but this **hope is in fact "tikvah" hope. Jesus is our only true hope in this world and for every person and for every nation.**

<u>HOPE GIVES TRUE MEANING TO LIFE - SOMETHING TO LIVE FOR...</u>
To have hope in Jesus results in the belief that my life is not worthless because God put me on this earth to be worthwhile. <u>The way to be worthwhile, is to do that which adds meaning and richness to the lives of others. Jesus set the example to us in this respect.</u>

"Tikvah"- hope is a rope that we can hang onto when the world seems out of control or when we don't know how to make it through a difficult season in life. Many of us have unfulfilled dreams, unaccomplished goals, half-built projects, and visions fading away into the past. We need to realize that God has the only unique plan for each one of us that fits our lives only.

Looking at the promise given to Israel, while they were captive in a strange and hostile land, illustrates God's loving, merciful character toward us: "For I know the thoughts that I think toward you, says the LORD, thoughts of peace, and not of evil, **to give you a future and a hope ("tikvah")".** Jeremiah 29:11.

"TIKVAH" HOPE, THE CHORD/ROPE TO CLING ONTO....
Yes, I can cling to God and cry out as the Psalmist did when he was in despair: **"For You are my hope ("tikvah"), O Lord GOD: You are my trust from my youth."** Psalm 71:5.
Here we see that hope and trust relate to each other. God is his hope/rope to cling to, with total expectation and assurance (trust) that He will save him.

In the story of Rahab in Joshua 2:17-18, it is illustrated how a hopeless situation becomes one of hope and the "rope" becomes a path to life in the circumstances of destruction. The rope was part of saving the Israelite spies from getting killed and the red rope became the answer to the salvation of Rahab and her family. According to the agreement, the Israelites would not wipe out Rahab and her family in the war. The sign of where they are was the red cord/rope that would hang out the window. The red rope/cord becomes a symbol of salvation and redemption for both parties.

"TIKVAH" HOPE IS ROOTED IN ACTIVELY WAITING

Romans 12:12 gives the principles in hoping: -
> It is to be joyful in the hope we have – the expectancy that, that which we hope for, will become reality. In this context we see that Rahab had joy in the hope that her family will be saved.
> Being patient amid uncertainty of the situation and circumstances while trusting in a faithful God of Hope.
> Praying and trusting in the one true God.... Rahab didn't even know this God of the Israelites, but she hoped in Him that He would be her and her family's salvation.

Rahab's hope was fulfilled, and she received what she hoped for. Her hope and faith in God also earned her a position in the earthly lineage of Jesus.

HOW DO WE PREVENT DOUBT FROM DESTROYING OUR HOPE?

Our "roots" must be anchored in a vital living relationship with Jesus and ourselves and secondly with others.
To illustrate this statement, we can observe the relationships in the story of Rahab and the Israelites.
> Rahab had to trust(hope) the spies to follow through with their promise to protect them in the time of war.
> The spies had to trust(hope) that Rahab would follow through with her promise to hide them (protect) and release them safely.
> Rahab had to wait and trust(hope) that the one true God whom she did not know at that moment, would be her salvation.
> Joshua needed assurance and trust(hope) in God when He said to Joshua "be strong and courageous and obedient (Joshua 1:18).

The active relationship with God of, especially the Israelites, in this specific incident, **became the key to the fulfillment of everyone's hope and trust.**

An active relationship with Jesus today, is also our "rope of hope" that we may cling to in times of despair and hopelessness. We can cling to, and depend on Him even when we can't see the next right step that we need to take. It is this hope and trust that also transforms our inner being under the hand of God.
When we relinquish our anxiety over to Him, we will find the hope that we long for amid the chaos. Our hope in Jesus then becomes our rest in Him through our faith in Him.
We need to realize that we can't trust and hope in our own abilities above the ability of Jesus in our lives. It is only Jesus that can calm the storm in our life.

HEBREWS 11:1-2 – HOPE AND FAITH

"Now <u>faith</u> is the <u>substance of things hoped for</u>, the <u>evidence of things not seen</u>. For by it the elders obtained a good report."
"Tikvah" (Hebrew Hope) and "Elpis" (Greek hope) become integrated in Hebrews 11 as the Old Testament history illustrates how hope and faith are intertwined with each other.
Hope resides in the unseen realm and can only be seen by faith and trust in God.
That is why faith is the "substance" of hope. The word "**<u>substance</u>**" in Greek ("hypostasis") has **the strong meaning of a "title deed"** with a further meaning of "**standing under the claim to the property to support its validity."** With this meaning in mind, we can see a much deeper meaning in Hebrews 11:1. **Faith is the "title deed" of the things hoped for... That which, though unseen, already exists beneath what is visible, that is our hope, but the "title deed" which is our faith, claims and confirms it by law as your property which includes your rights of ownership. Faith defines hope and makes the expected unseen a reality in**

our mind, which leads us to the actions that fits our expectation. When our hope and faith is aligned with the will of God, we will experience the fulfilment thereof.
This is also described in Romans 8:24-25

Let's hope, trust, and believe in the spoken Word of God and find our strength and power in His grace, mercy, and love which He equips us with to be able to carry on in difficult times.

REMEMBER: -

In our own strength we will fail.
Focusing on the storm of negative circumstances
weakens us and destroys our faith,
leading us further into destruction.
Our salvation, strength, and faith
must be rooted in Jesus Christ who is our "Rope of Hope"
which we must cling onto
through maintaining our relationship with Him.
Let's be sensitive to His guidance
and follow in His footsteps
according to His Word in obedience
and experience His abundance of blessings
that He has in store for us.
....And we will overcome in His power, not our own.

THE BROKEN VESSEL

"God turns broken vessels into vessels of honour"
as said by Pastor Reinhardt Bonke

For Catherine, the day started early in the summer. Tensions are running high in the house. The children are slow to co-operate, and the thunder clouds are thickly packed between her and her husband. It's been a few years now that the various incidents, some small and others big, have been systematically dismantling their marriage and family life and it's as if Catherine just can't do anything right to improve matters anymore.

With another cry to her Heavenly Father in her upset heart, just to help things get right, Catherine hurried with the children to the car to start another workday. Fortunately, her husband has already driven to work, and this tension is temporarily off her shoulders. Yet her heart is loaded with misfortune and the tears are piled up behind her heart's dam wall, ready to break under the pressure at any moment. She hurriedly climbed in behind the steering wheel and discovered a handwritten letter pasted onto the middle of the steering wheel.

"It's finished, I don't love you anymore. You have let my love for you die. I want a divorce. You will soon get the divorce letters. Never kiss me again or try to hug me, don't touch me again." It hits Catherine like a message of the death of a loved one. Her whole life is finally crumbling in front of her mind's eye, and everything is being ruined in one moment. All the memories, good and bad play off like a quick film in front of her. No hope, no future, just a sword hanging over her head, threatening to ruin her and her children's lives. "Lord, please help me..." she prays softly, as she continues like any other day, without allowing the upset situation to prevail, driving to work and school. She can't tell the kids about this issue right now. She must first reflect and try to put all the pieces of her life together so that she can still mean "something" to her children. One thing is certain, without a gracious and loving God in her life, she could not move one step further....

So much injustice, so much resentment and disappointment. It's a crisis you can't flee from, because even in the loneliness of your room, away from all the circumstances, the emotional pain pierces your heart, like when someone pierces you with a dagger. An abundance of "whys" comes down into your confused thoughts and nothing you do, can yield it orderly or give satisfying answers. Between the sobs and pains, there is only one cry for help that you know can change your life's struggles, and it is the cry towards your Heavenly Father and Creator that holds the future, you, and your family's lives in the hollow of His hand.

This is just another chapter from the true reality of many women and even men's lives. The pain and trauma of life often triggered by the devastating hand of Satan are evident in almost every human being. When the profound life crises come knocking on our door, we have a choice to deal with them positively with God, or to fall into the negative traumatic, devastating circumstances without God.

When your life lies in shattered, broken pieces at your feet, you are brought to a standstill with a shock, to reflect again on all that you are, everything you have been until now, and everything you are likely to become in the future.

In times like these, the way you and I respond, is the determining factor that will permanently affect our entire lives. **It's not what happens to you, but how you react to it, that counts.**

Some of us are going to remain at this crisis that has shattered everything. We can't move on. We scramble around to get all the bits of our life together and effort in vain. Putting it back together ourselves, only results in having to live with lasting emotional, mental, and sometimes physical trauma. Another person will just sit there among all the broken pieces, watching with despair as the rest of the pieces of their life are further trampled and crushed by the indifference of humanity. Then there are those who sit down at the feet of Jesus in their brokenness, so that He can pick up the pieces of their lives and restore their spirit and soul and make their lives new by His grace, mercy, and love.

In which category will you place yourself? Where do you stand in life versus your crises and toward God?

From the very beginning, the Lord has built a promise of healing into His plan for mankind. He, more than any other being or creature, has a deep understanding of the profound trauma of spirit, soul, and body caused by our wrong decisions, by sin, and by the convergence of circumstances. Satan delights in slaughtering, destroying, killing, and robbing our lives from any form of true happiness and love. He wants to draw us as far away from God as it is within his sick ability and convince us that God is not the answer to our problems.

Thank the Lord for His power, that He is always in control, even though everything seems humanly speaking, out of control!

When the crises of life have tapped every ounce of our spiritual, emotional, and physical energy, we read in Isaiah 42:3 that He does not break or crush the bruised reed, nor quench the dim wick. How merciful our God is to us! He does not trample and crush us, when it seems that we cannot be of any more value to life. No, He heals and renews us and binds up our heart's wounds, healing our brokenness. Psalm 147:3.

Psalm 145:14 tells us that the Lord supports us when we are falling and lifts us up when we are bent over. When we are weighed down by the burdens of worry and pain, it is Jesus Himself who invites us to come and lay down our burdens at His feet, when he tells us: " Come unto Me, all you that labor and are heavy laden, and I will give you rest. Take My yoke upon you and learn of Me; for I am meek and lowly in heart: and ye shall find rest unto your souls. For my yoke is easy, and my burden is light." See Matthew 11:28-30.

The emotional and spiritual trauma of this life often leaves deep lasting scars and can even cause us to have permanent emotional disability. If we do not humble ourselves before the Lord and begin to forgive everyone who has hurt us in pain and sorrow, we will have permanent spiritual, emotional and on the long term, physical disabilities. **Just as the Lord fully forgives you, every sin and injustice you have committed, God is now asking you to forgive every person who has harmed you, without expecting any apology from them. Jesus tells us this in Matthew 6:14-15. Forgiveness cannot be earned but is given from a wounded but sincerely obedient heart. A heart that is willing to trust and obey God in every way, no matter how dire the circumstances, you will experience salvation from the bondage of bitterness and hatred. Forgiveness and justification become the keys to the healing of your own broken life.**

As Jesus hung for our sins in the greatest pain and desolation on the cross and was unjustly tortured, He cried out: **"Father, forgive them, for they do not know what they are doing!"** Luke 23:34.

Jesus came to teach us this path of forgiveness and justification in the true sense of the word, but He also came to free us from the bondage of bitterness, rejection, inferiority, hatred, and depression that often leads to suicide. In Isaiah 61:1-3,10 we find that He frees us by His Spirit and sets us free from our spiritual imprisonment, He gives us the oil of joy, turns mourning into praise, and clothes us in a garment of righteousness. He comforts those who sit in brokenness and revives the crushed hearted. It is God Himself who heals us again, as defined in Isaiah 57:15,18.

He promises not to leave you but to carry you through and give you the ability to go on again, thinking of you every moment, because your name is engraved in His hand palm.
Read Isaiah 46:3,4 & Isaiah 49:15b–16.

When a crisis of life brings us to a standstill, it is also time to allow God to speak to us through His Spirit. Often it is necessary to allow His Spirit to also show us the weaknesses and hidden sins in our own lives. It is not a pleasant moment, but an opportunity to be cleansed and purified by the blood of Jesus through confession. Abba Father promises in Isaiah 43:25 that He will clear out all our transgressions and never think about them again. It is on this occasion that our lives become soft like clay in the hands of the Potter, and He can mold our life according to His will, useful for His glory. In 2 Timothy 2:20,21, we are encouraged to cleanse ourselves so that we may be a vessel to God's glory, useful in His hands.

Jeremiah reminds us in Jeremiah 29:11 that God plans prosperity for us, not evil. We need to surrender our lives fully to Him so that His plans for us can be fulfilled.

God exhorts us in Isaiah 43:18 that we should not remember the former things but put the past behind us. Jesus repeats this exhortation in Luke 9:62 when He tells us that no one is fit for the kingdom of God if he continues to look backwards as he plows forward. When we focus on shutting down the past and stretching ourselves out to what Jesus has stored in our future for us, we will taste the true life and prosperity He has for us. In Isaiah 43:19, He promises us a new life, for He makes a path in our spiritual wilderness and pours out His living waters of His Spirit-laden Word upon us so that we will again be able to bear new divine fruit. Isaiah 44:2a,3.

Inner healing does not happen in an instant, but when God touches us, we can be assured that He is working a perfect work within us. He is not only near the brokenhearted, as stated in Psalm 34:19, but turns their wailing into dancing and removes your sackcloth so that He may gird you with a robe of joy as defined in Psalm 30:12.

When a rose is crushed, after being trampled upon, its fragrance emerges strongly. The greatest sacrifice we can make to God in our most broken moments is our broken lives. Psalm 51:19 says, "The sacrifices of God are a broken spirit; "You will not despise a broken and contrite heart, O God." It will go up before Him like an incense offering.

There have been several attempts to restore this unhappy marriage of Catherine, but alas, they are divorced. A new life has begun for all the parties of this family. From a human point of view, there was nothing to look forward to except hardship and wrestling to keep head above water. Catherine learned how absolutely faithful God is to His Word, where He promises in John 10:28-30 that He holds us tight and that nothing and no one can snatch us out of His hands. In the most difficult of times, God's provision and guidance were evident in her and that of her family's life.

Catherine continued to serve God and trust Him to repair the emotional pain and spiritual trauma in her and that of her children's lives. The Lord works this in a miraculous way that she receives help from a pastoral counselor. A God-given healing process of spirit, soul and body begins in her life and even takes place as far back as her childhood. She experiences how the Lord makes her broken life whole and new again; how her life of all that dishonors Him is purified and how His Spirit wonderfully drenched her life anew with God's presence. Her children also had a life-changing experience through His healing process.

Abba Father was faithful to His Word. He answered her prayers of supplications, saw her tears, her abandonment, and brokenness. He was faithful to His promise in Isaiah 62:3-5.
He picked her up in His mercy, grace, and love, carried her in His arms, and turned every bit of trauma into a spiritual victory. He refreshed her weary and dwindling soul again. Read Jeremiah 31:25.

In His love, the Lord drew Catherine near to Him, built her up into a new woman, and adorned her with joy. He leveled her life paths again, giving her the streams of water of His Spirit-laden Word within her.

Catherine found a new hope in Jesus and discovered a new vision for her and her family's life. Her focus now more than ever was on Jesus, the Beginning and Finisher of her faith, as defined in Hebrews 12:2. Her heart couldn't help but cry out: **"Lord, you are truly Great and Wonderful! Your touch has changed my life forever!"**

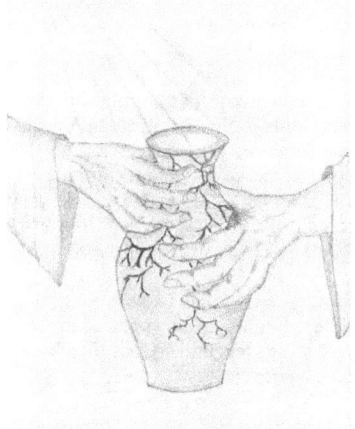

"As confirmation of the inner healing of spirit and soul, the Lord showed me a "picture" of a broken vessel/pitcher, which represented my life. It was empty and full of cracks, not useful for anything. It would not be able to carry water. He placed His hands on either side of the vessel and as it turned around on the potter's table, between His hands, while moving gently over it, every crack began to disappear, and the vessel became whole again. He said, "You are in My hands and as the potter forms something new out of the clay, so I will make you new again." Isaiah 53:5 & Jeremiah 18:4,6"

"She experienced how Abba Father continued the healing process in her heart and life and how Jesus wrapped her in a blanket of His eternal love and comfort. A new picture began to unfold... Her life is whole again — no more cracks. His hand rests lovingly on her, throwing seeds inside her vessel/pitcher. He said, "Behold, I love you with a perfect love, for you are Mine. You are My daughter, and My kingdom seed is implanted in your heart and in your life to bear fruit for My glory. I've started something new in you, look, it's already sprouting. It will leave a path of life in the wilderness of life, and many will walk on it and be satisfied." Isaiah 43:19,20 & 2 Corinthians 4:6,7."

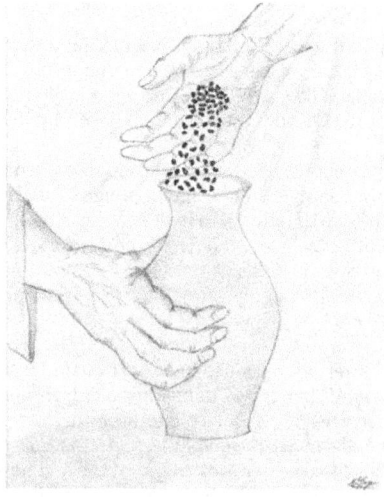

Abba Father restored this broken vessel and turned it into a vessel of honor. One that is useful in His hands.

What is your crisis today? What are you going to do with it?

Our Heavenly Father wants to help you but waits for you to make the important choice in which you make Him part of your life's struggles. It's a choice in which you submit to the working of His powerful and loving hand in your life. A choice to obey your Almighty Heavenly Father.
Like Catherine, you too can receive healing. You are safe in God's hands.

Remember: - "... For those who love God, all things work together for good, for those who are called according to His purpose."
Romans 8:28.

EVERY CLOUD MOST CERAINLY HAS A GOLDEN EDGE

Revelation 1:7
"Look! He is returning with the clouds,
and every eye will see Him,
even those who pierced Him,
and all the tribes on the earth will mourn because of Him."
This will certainly come to pass!
Amen."

One day the clouds will roll away as one will fold open a scroll and Christ will stand before us in His full glory. WOW! What a breathtaking moment!! Are you ready to meet Him in this way? He promised to come back to get His children. Read about it in John 14:1-3.

In the meantime, He has much to reveal to us and we should not see the clouds as signs of His absence. It is the clouds that remind us that Jesus is coming back to fetch us.

In the Bible, God is many times associated with clouds. Clouds are often a sign of sorrow, suffering, or circumstances that the Lord allows in or around our lives, those things that seem to contradict the omnipotence of God. Yet it is because of these very clouds that the Holy Spirit of God teaches us how-to walk-in faith. When the clouds of circumstance sometimes gather thickly around us, it becomes difficult to see the hand of God in them and we are compelled to trust God blindly. If there are never clouds in our lives, we will not develop faith.

The Bible describes in various places God's "symbolic connection" with the clouds.
Clouds are the dust under our Heavenly Father's feet... as described in Nahum 1:3 and sometimes He makes the clouds His chariot with which He meets us. According to Psalm 104:3. Sometimes it is in the cloud, where we, like Moses, meet with God.... Read about it in Exodus 24:16-18. The clouds are a sign that God is there. For Israel, the fiery cloud announced God's presence and protection, and without this cloud, Moses wanted to move no further.... As described in Exodus 33:15-17.

Through every cloud He brings over our path, He wants us to learn something. His purpose in the clouds is to simplify what we believe until our relationship with Him is like that of a child. A relationship simply between God and our own spirit where other people are nothing more than shadows... Until we can face some of the deepest, darkest truths of life, without changing our view of God's character. It is in these moments that we fully realize the true reality of God's promise to us when He tells us: **"I will never leave you nor forsake you.** " Hebrews 13:5.

Sometimes the clouds are not dark but prevent you from seeing clearly and lead to your circumstances confusing you. Even if we cannot see the end of our life path, even if the future looks bleak, we can **only blindly trust God and follow step by step in His footsteps**. Soon we will also be able to declare: **"The Lord is my Helper, and I will not** fear... " as said in Hebrews 13:6. It is then that you pray and rest in faith and in God's grace, for soon His Light will break through the clouds and you will know that God has always hold your hand very tightly.... As Jesus tells us in John 10:28,29.

Often, the dark clouds hold a promise of life-giving rain. Remember, when God's life-giving Spirit fulfills spoken Word as His rain settles on you, you will be truly blessed.

Look out for your Lord and your God who is coming in the clouds, living with an expectation to see Him! He is truly our God of hope!

*"For just like the lightning comes from the east and flashes to the west,
so, the coming of the Son of Man (Jesus) will be.
Then the sign of the Son of Man (Jesus) will appear in heaven,
and all the tribes of the earth will mourn.
They will see the Son of Man (Jesus) arriving on the clouds of heaven
with power and great glory."
Matthew 24:27,30*

v.   YOU, O GOD, ARE TRULY THE ALPHA AND OMEGA!

Revelation 1:8
"I am the Alpha and the Omega," says the Lord God –
the One who is, and who was, and who is still to come –
the All-Powerful!"

WHO OR WHAT IS YOUR ALPHA AND OMEGA?

Revelation 1:8
"I am the Alpha and the Omega," says the Lord God –
the One who is, and who was, and who is still to come –
the All-Powerful!"

Already from birth there is an unconscious need to fill the spiritual emptiness within us. God already fills us at birth with a measure of His life-giving Spirit the moment we give that first breath. After that, it is part of our Divine mission to discover Him as our Creator, Abba Father, and Savior.

Since many people in this modern age do not practice and have a living relationship with God, our offspring grow up without a relationship with the True Living God. As a result, many fill this spiritual void with all sorts of erroneous teachings and dogmas to try to get fulfillment. These include all kinds of pagan practices and religions as well as drug abuse and alcohol abuse and many more...

When we discover the Lord in spirit and truth and allow Him to come and take residence in us, worship Him, and walk in His will, our spiritual fulfillment begins to become a reality. It becomes the starting point to start living out the divine plan God has for our lives. It is also the real starting point for true lasting fulfillment and happiness.

The Lord says in Isaiah 44:6: "... **I AM THE FIRST (ALPHA) AND I AM THE LAST.**"
In Genesis 1, we see how the Spirit of God, in other words, God Himself, is hovering/" brooding" over the waters of the earth. Through the speaking of His powerful Word, He creates a whole new earth within six days. Everything is perfect, and in orderly synchronizing with each other.

The Hebrew word for "God" in this passage is "Elohim/ Eloheem" (H430) which has a multiple/plural connotation to it. The reason for this is to emphasize the power, greatness, and His sovereignty. He is and remains a "Supreme God" as one of the explanations in H430 emphasizes it.

God is Spirit (see John 4:24) and when He speaks, He brings life into being. In His power, His Word never returns to Him unfulfilled and empty. His word carries authority and power! Read about this in Isaiah 55:8-11.

Jesus repeatedly describes and identifies Himself as the **ALPHA AND OMEGA, THE FIRST AND THE LAST** in Revelation 1:11; Revelation 2:8; Revelation 22:13. From this we can determine that God and Jesus are in fact ONE and the same; God's Name is also called, Jesus. **Genesis 1 marks the beginning for us on earth, according to God's Word, the Bible, even though He existed before that time.**

In the Old Testament, in Isaiah 43:10-11, God also confirms that He is Alpha and Omega with these words: "You are my witnesses, says the Lord, and My servant whom I have chosen, that you may know and believe Me and understand that I am He**; before Me there was no God formed, and after Me there will be none. I, even I, am the Lord, and besides Me there is no savior.**" The Lord goes on to say in Isaiah 44:6: "**... I am the first and I am the last, and besides Me there is no God.**" In His capacity as Creator, Father, Savior, and King, the Lord says in verse 24: "Thus says the Lord your Redeemer, and He that formed you from the womb: ' I am Jehovah, the One doing all things, the One who is laying forth the heavens, I alone, and the One spreading out the earth, who has been with Me?' —" In Isaiah 45:21-24, God declares these wonderful words: "... **And besides Me there is no other God, a just and saving God besides Me.** Turn to Me and be saved, all the ends of the earth. For I **am God, and there is no other.** I swear by Myself; **Righteousness proceeds out of My mouth, a word that is not revoked: that before Me every knee shall bow,** every tongue shall swear (affirm). They will say about Me, "Yes, the LORD is a powerful Deliverer...

There is also no place for other gods in your relationship with the Lord. In Isaiah 48:11b, God says clearly. "- For My sake alone I will act, for how can I allow my Name to be defiled? **I will not share my glory with anyone else!"**
 Isaiah 46:9 tells us that there should be no other God in our lives because He alone is God.:
 "...Truly I am God, I have no peer; **I am God, and there is none like Me,** who **announces the end from the beginning and reveals beforehand what has not yet occurred,** who says, 'My plan will be realized, I will accomplish what I desire",

From these passages we see that God is an only God, not only numerically one, but also one in essence. We see how **He is the <u>First/Alpha</u> and <u>Last/Omega</u> in the <u>Old Testament</u>, and He bears the same qualities in the New Testament.** He was and is and will be...

<u>... OMEGA - THE LAST, THE END</u>?
We know the end within context of our earthly existence. God does NOT have an end to His existence because He is eternal. **He does add an end to things in the universe and to mankind according to His divine plan.** Revelation reminds us of eternal life after earthly death that is, if we are a child of God and live within His will and love.

A true encounter with God leads to, not only being changed forever, but that God Himself becomes the Alpha and Omega of your entire existence. It becomes the beginning of an intense love affair with the King of all kings, your Creator, your Abba Father. **It is this intense love for God that becomes the driving force of your existence and brings fulfillment of that spiritual void.** Romans 5:5 says that the Holy Spirit pours out God's love in our hearts so that we may love Him and our fellow man as He commanded us.
John 14:15 says, "If you love Me, keep My commandments." ("Commandments" here are defined in G1785 – "ethole" –meaning authoritarian precepts of Jesus). Jesus said in John 14:21-23,
<u>"He who has My commandments and keeps them is he who loves Me.</u> And he that loves Me shall be loved of my Father, and I will love him, and will manifest Myself unto him.
"Jesus replied, "If anyone **loves Me,** he will **obey My word**, and My Father will love him, and we will come to him **and take up residence with him."** **The word "obey/keep"** in the above verses is defined **in Greek in G5083** with the meaning of "**do**", "**fulfill**". <u>Our obedience to Jesus' authoritarian precepts is a prerequisite for our love for Him. Here we see how Love for God and obedience take hands as a demonstration of our love for Jesus</u>. It has a wonderful **result**, namely, that **Jesus comes to dwell with us, and He reveals Himself to us by His Spirit.**

Have you ever had a specific day in which Jesus became your Alpha and Omega? Have you made Jesus, the King of all kings the beginning and end of YOUR existence?

"He has told you, O man, what is good,
and what the LORD really wants from you:
He wants you to promote justice, to be faithful,
and to live obediently before your God.
Micah 6:8
"But if someone loves God, he is known by God."
1 Corinthians 8:3

WHO IS THE GOD YOU & I BELIEVE IN AND WORSHIP?

Deuteronomy 6:4-7
"Hear, O Israel: The LORD our God is one LORD:
And you shall love the LORD your God with all your heart,
and with all your soul, and with all your might.
And these words, which I command you this day, shall be in your heart:
And you shall teach them diligently unto your children,
and shall talk of them when you sit in your house, and
when you walk by the way, and when you lie down, and when you rise up."

We have already seen clearly in the previous writing how there is **only ONE God** whom we should worship, serve, and love, moreover, that this **God is ONE** and does not have 3 separate personalities. We need to **discern WHO the God is that we are worshipping**? Is He truly the God of the Bible, or is he a "fantasy" made up out of our own perceptions? What we see in the Bible, is what we should accept as the truth and there is one specific fact we must remember and dwell on, which is - **As He is the First and the Last in Isaiah, so He is the First and the Last in Revelation.**

To further confirm these statements, let's look at the Scripture with which we started this writing: "Hear, O Israel: The LORD our **God is one LORD**: And you shall **love the LORD** your God with **all your heart**, and with **all your soul**, and with **all your might**.
And these words, which I command you this day, shall be in your heart: And you shall teach them diligently unto your children, and shall talk of them when you sit in your house, and when you walk by the way, and when you lie down, and when you rise up."
Deuteronomy 6:4-7.
When we look at the original meaning of the word "one" at H259, we see the Hebrew word used here is "echad", which has a meaning of' numerically one" or "properly (united) all of one/first". This accommodates the possibility that a "composite" one as defined in the Trinity theology which originally originated from the "Nicene Creed" formulated around 300 AD by the Catholic church fathers may well be the truth. **But God is faithful not to contradict Himself, but rather to reaffirm His Word in the Bible that carries far more power than any human formula or statement.** Let's look at what **Jesus says in Mark 12:29-31**. Jesus is asked by the scribes what the first commandment is. "And Jesus said unto him, the first of all the commandments is: "Hear, O Israel: The LORD our **God is one LORD**: And you shall **love the LORD** your God with **all your heart**, and with **all your soul**, and with **all your might**. And these words, which I command you this day, shall be in your heart: And you shall teach them diligently unto your children, and shall talk of them when you sit in your house, and when you walk by the way, and when you lie down, and when you rise up."
And the second is like, namely this, you shall love your neighbor as yourself. There is none other commandment greater than these.

When we look at the Greek meaning of the word "one" at G1520, we see the word spoken here by Jesus is "heis" with the primary meaning of numerically ONE meaning God is essentially ONE.

WHY DO WE READ ABOUT GOD AS OUR FATHER, OF JESUS AS THE SON AND THE HOLY SPIRIT SEPARATELY?
Remember that Jesus came to earth as a Hebrew, and Israel saw and came to know God in Hebrew context. Israel was God's chosen people and revealed Himself to them in various ways. So, what would that mean?

Hebrew thinking occurred predominantly **within context of <u>functionality</u>**, and it is still so in practice. The **Greek thinking** is guided in context of the **<u>physical reality and form</u>** and NOT functional. For example, **it was and is "functional" for God to act at different appropriate times according to His Divine plan, as Father, as Son and Holy Spirit, and so reveal Himself, but this did not make Him a "plural God with three distinct personalities."**

Example of functional conduct in everyday life: A man can **be a husband to his wife** within the context of marriage, be **a father to** his children, and be an **engineer** at his job. **Still, he remains ONE person with different functionalities.**

As I had to reform in my heart and mind around this fact, that God is ONE, based on the truth in His Word — the Bible, and was praying about it, I heard in my spirit how God clearly said: **"I am NOT a god with a split multiple personality as with the abnormality of "multiple personality disorder"!!**
I am God, and besides Me there is no other! No other personalities, no, I am ONE"

God reveals Himself through various visible manifestations **in the <u>Old Testament</u>,** but remains Spirit, as Jesus declared in John 4:24.
In the **Old Testament** we see how:
- ❖ He visited Adam and Eve in the garden of Eden in the evening breeze – Genesis 3:8.
- ❖ We see Him leading Israel with the pillar of cloud and pillar of fire as defined in Exodus.
- ❖ He reveals Himself on Mount Sinai in fire, lightning and thunder with trumpet sound as defined in Exodus 19:18-21; God reveals Himself in His greatness, during a "visit" on the mountain, where Moses, the elders and Aaron and his two sons, were present. Read about it in Exodus 24:10-11.
- ❖ God reveals His majesty in Spirit and at the same time in human form on a throne to Ezekiel in Ezekiel 1.
- ❖ To Daniel, God reveals Himself as the "Ancient of Days" at Daniel 7:9,22 and much more....

<u>Yet God remains ONE and the same in His essence and personality. God is Spirit and therefore He can reveal Himself in these ways</u>.

In the <u>New Testament</u>, we see even more how God reveals and manifests Himself in a functional way:
- ❖ It was necessary for God to become man in the form of Jesus so that He could bring about eternal perfect salvation for mankind for those who receive Him.
- ❖ At the same time, Jesus was begotten by God's Spirit in Mary, making Him the Son of God, but also the Son of Man.
- ❖ After Jesus was crucified and rose again, He returned to His heavenly place and also came to take residence in the heart and spirit of His followers and children through His Spirit. Through His Spirit He can reveal Himself in more than one person and thus establish His Kingdom on earth.

<u>DOES THAT SOUND INCREDIBLE? LET'S TAKE A CLOSER LOOK AT THESE FACTS THROUGH THE "GLASSES" OF THE PROPHETIC WORD OF ISAIAH 9:6:</u>
Isaiah9:6 foretells the **<u>coming of Jesus as God, but also as a Son, to this earth</u>**, saying: "For unto us **a child is born, a Son is given; and the government shall be upon His shoulder, and His name shall be called <u>Wonderful, Counselor, Mighty God, Everlasting Father, Prince of Peace</u>—**" Pay close attention to these five names. **It not only reveals God's character, but also indicates that Jesus Himself is our God.** Isaiah 7:14 says, **"Therefore the Lord Himself will give you a sign: 'Look, the virgin will conceive and bear a son and will call His name**

Emmanuel.' This prophetic word is used in Matthew 1:23 with the meaning of the name "Emmanuel" which is **"GOD WITH US."**
Emmanuel means that this son and child, also called Mighty God and Everlasting Father, is the God referred to in Matthew 1:23, as "God with us." He came to live among us and walk with us with a specific purpose. The **purpose was salvation, redemption, grace as well as the announcement of a "new" way of life according to Divine Kingdom principles drenched with love for God and our neighbor. A new Way, a new Truth and new Life in and through Jesus Christ our Lord according to John 14:6.**

When we confess that Jesus (Yeshua) Christ (the Anointed One) came in the flesh, we are actually referring to the fact that the Mighty God and Everlasting Father was clothed with flesh.

The spirit of Antichrist disowns the above facts in the Bible by stating that there is an extra father besides the one from Isaiah 9:6, who did not come in the flesh, which is also part of the Godhead.

WHAT WE NEED TO UNDERSTAND AND REALIZE IS THAT **JESUS HAD TWO NATURES, NAMELY:**
1.   He was human (child and son) and
2.   He was God the Father (Mighty God and Everlasting Father).

In other words, God/Jesus is a Spirit being within a fleshly body — at the same time, Father and Son.
❖   Jesus was 100% a man (child and son).
❖   100% God (Mighty God and Everlasting Father).

It is in view of this that Jesus said in John 14:10 that **the Father who is within Him does** the works and that He cannot do anything of Himself. This truth is further confirmed by Paul when he writes to the congregation of Colossians in Colossians 2:9: **"For in Him (Jesus) dwelleth all the fullness of the Godhead bodily; "** John also confirms this fact when he says in 1 John 5:20: **"And we know that the Son of God is come, and hath given us an understanding, that we may know Him that is true, and we are in Him that is true, even in His Son Jesus Christ. This is the true God, and eternal life."**

Let us therefore worship the one true God and Lord
in spirit and truth.
And we certainly know the truth.
As He reveals it to us
Through His Spirit.
Amen

THE "LOGOS" WORD OF GOD

John 1:1-3,14
"In the beginning was the Word,
and the Word was with God,
and the Word was God.
The same was in the beginning with God.
All things were made by Him;
and without Him was not anything made that was made.

And the Word was made flesh,
and dwelt among us, (and we beheld His glory,
the glory as of the only begotten of the Father,)
full of grace and truth."

We then build on the last two writings to improve our insight and understanding regarding the Godhead even deeper.

Re-read the text as shown above.
"In the beginning was the **Word...**" The Greek language used here is **"Logos"** – G3056, which has the following meaning – thinking, thoughts of the mind; motive and reasoning ability, as well as planning. That means it was part of God's logical thinking and planning from the beginning to come to earth in fleshly form. Is this said somewhere else in the Bible? Yes, of course! As far back as Genesis 3:15 where the coming of Jesus—God in the flesh— was pronounced and foretold by God Himself.

John affirms that **God's logical thinking, which resulted in His divine plan,** was already with God from the beginning and that it would **become reality through His spoken Word.**
Just as one's words and thoughts does not represent another person, **so the words and thoughts of God are not another person, but inherently His own personal Divine thoughts.**
God's spoken Word carries indescribably great creative power, so we see in John 1:14 that God's Word/planned thoughts became flesh in the form of Jesus. Verse 14 says, "And the **Word become flesh** and dwelt among us, and we **beheld His glory,** the glory as of the only begotten of the Father, full of grace and truth."
There is more in the original meaning of G3056 – **"Logos"** which includes the following: **"The Divine Expression (that is Jesus Christ), the reality of the Godly thoughts – account, caused through communication."** What God had planned in His mind from the beginning, was with Him, and became a visible reality, from His spoken Word in the form of Jesus Christ.

When we look attentively at the question Phillip asked Jesus, together with what Jesus answered him, our insight concerning the Godhead will change dramatically. We read in John 14:8-10: "Philip said, "Lord, **show us the Father,** and we will be content." Jesus replied, **"Have I been with you for so long, and you have not known Me,** Philip? **The person who has seen Me has seen the Father!** How can you say, 'Show us the Father'? Do you not **believe that I am in the Father, and the Father is in Me**? The words that I say to you, I do not speak on my own initiative, **but the Father residing in Me performs His miraculous deeds."**
Jesus explains how the Father is in the Son. If the Father was in the Son at that time, then only the Father became flesh, which is in line with Isaiah 9:6.

Let's look at 1 John 5:20 again: ""**And we know that the <u>Son of God is come</u>, and hath <u>given us an understanding</u>, that <u>we may know Him</u> that is true, and <u>we are in Him that is true</u>, *even* in His Son <u>Jesus Christ. This is the true God, and eternal life."</u>**
Three important points concerning this verse are the following: -
1.   The reason the Son of God came, was to give us understanding of God so that we might know Him.
2.   So, we can understand with our minds who God really is.
3.   Jesus is the true God and eternal life.

The spirit of Antichrist does not want to acknowledge that the "fullness of the Godhead" has become flesh. This is exactly the opposite of what Colossians 2:9 tells us. He will try to convince you that God is too great to understand with our limited mind. The Antichrist spirit also says that God's Son became flesh, implying that only a third of God was involved in the salvation of man which is a false account of the true Gospel of Jesus Christ. Do not forget that the Name "Jesus" /"Yeshua," means "Jehovah our Savior."

Just a reminder: There are two dimensions revealed in Isaiah 9:6:
1.   The natural human child and son.
2.   The spiritual God and Father.

Colossians 2:9 confirms this fact "For **in Him (Jesus) dwells all the fulness of the Godhead bodily**. Paul also wrote to Timothy in 1 Timothy 2:9: "For **there is one God** and one Mediator between God and men, **the man Christ Jesus**."

God is Spirit and His Spirit is the Father as defined in Matthew 1:18: "The birth of Jesus Christ was thus: When his mother Mary was betrothed to Joseph before they came together, she was **found pregnant by the Holy Spirit."**

<u>NOTICE THE FOLLOWING PASSAGES OF SCRIPTURE REGARDING JESUS' "POSITION":</u>
1 Corinthians 12:3 – Jesus is Lord
2 Corinthians 3:17 The Lord is the Spirit
Ephesians 4:5 – There is just ONE Lord
There is only ONE Lord in the Old Testament and ONE Lord in the New Testament who has clothed Himself with flesh to give mankind a chance for true salvation.

We see that it was "functional" for God to walk on earth as a fleshly entity and bring about our salvation and redemption. It was and is also "functional" that His fullness through His Spirit dwells in us who have accepted Him and through regeneration (being born again) He becomes our Everlasting Father anew. Please read about this in James 1:18,21 and 1 John 3:8-9.

When Jesus returns at the second coming, we see in Zechariah 14:5b,9 the following: "... Then shall the LORD my God come, and all the saints with thee. And the LORD shall be king over all the earth. In THAT DAY **THE LORD WILL BE ONE, AND HIS NAME ONE."**
Here we see how the "functionality" of different "entities" will no longer be necessary since the Ecclesia believers (saved crowd) will always be in His direct presence in heaven because they have inherited eternal life.

Let us never forget **that God is Spirit and that those who worship Him should worship Him in spirit and truth,** according to John 4:24.

The Lord Himself says this on that great and wonderful day that He is coming again, in Revelation 3,7: "And I heard a great voice from heaven **saying, Behold, the tabernacle of God is with men, and He shall dwell with them, and they shall be His people; And God Himself** will be with them as their God. He that overcomes shall inherit all things; and I will be his God, and he shall be my son."

I conclude with the words of Jesus in *Revelation 22:12-14:* -

"(Look! I am coming soon,
and My reward is with Me to pay each one
according to what he has done!
I am the Alpha and the Omega,
the first and the last,
the beginning and the end!)

Blessed are those who wash their robes
so they can have access
to the tree of life and
can enter into the city by the gates."

DISCOVER THE CHARACTER OF GOD BETWEEN THE PAGES OF THE BIBLE AND EXPERIENCE HIS AWESOME GREATNESS

We see how the people of the Old and New Testaments link their personal experience to a fitting character trait that depicts their experience with the Lord. In this way, we see that many names are linked to Him. In this way, the essence of who God is, is revealed. Even though there are many names attached to Him, we are still assured of Only, One Living God's existence that is unchanging in His ways. So, He provides us with an anchor and steadfastness in a variable, uncertain world.

God is limitless and His existence is certain!
He is the Alpha and Omega of all that exists.
He is Ruler and King of the Universe...

God progressively revealed Himself to the people of the **Old Testament** by His Name. Exodus 3:14 says, "God says to **Moses, 'I AM WHO I AM.'** He says, "Thus shall you say unto the children of Israel, **I AM, have sent me unto you."**

Exodus 6:1-2 "God spoke to Moses and said to him, **"I am the LORD"** (H3068). And I appeared to Abraham, to Isaac, and to Jacob as **Almighty God,** but by My Name **"Jehovah" (YHWH)** I did not make Myself known to them." **His Name reveals His authority, His character, and the fact that He is truly a Reality.** "YHWH" is linked to a Hebrew meaning of "**to be"** and is pronounced like as if taking a breath. He is as close as every breath we take. After all, God breathed His breath into man so that man could become a living soul as we read about it in Genesis 2:7. **This breath is part of God's life-giving Spirit** as Job describes it in Job 33:4 and Job 34:14-15.

On this foundation, that **"God is YHWH,"** Israel and Moses were able to build their lives. They get to know God as the God in whom they can trust and lean on; God is merciful and full of grace, who provides, heals, and protects. Within the confines of His will, they will enjoy His blessing and prosperity. Yet today they and we must remember that He is holy and to be feared, not a fear that makes you anxious, but the kind of fear that brings absolute dignity, honor, and respectful wonder to Him, which makes us want to worship Him in spirit and truth. The word for this "wonder/admiration" for God is," reverence" and is described as a "**Reverential feeling of deep respect or awe, including the realization that God is present at every moment: seeing your every thought and deed. In fact, your whole being is "transparent" to Him"**

GOD PROGRESSIVELY REVEALS HIMSELF IN ALL HIS FACETS AND SO AFFIRMS HIS TRUE ACTIVE EXISTENCE.
Let's look at some of these unique character traits: -
Adam comes to know God as His **Creator and Father** (Please read Luke 3:38**b**) and after the fall into sin, as **a gracious and merciful God**. Why? Because God had the choice and power to wipe them out in His wrath when they did not obey Him, but the Lord opened a way to salvation as we see in Genesis 3:14,21, onward.

After these events, we see that a man named Enoch had such an intense relationship with God that the Bible tells us, Enoch walked with God and God took him up into heaven to be with Him. We can read about this in Genesis 5:24.

We discover how Noah caught God's attention by remaining faithful to God amid an extremely wicked world. The Bible describes Noah as a righteous, upright man who walked with God. We read about this in Genesis 6:9-22. God saves this family from certain death in the flood because they served and honored Him.

To Abraham, He is more than **Almighty God ("El Shaddai"),** as defined in Genesis 17:1, He is also **"Jehovah-Jireh" meaning "The Lord will provide."** We read of this experience of Abraham in Genesis 22:14.

We read in Genesis 16:13 how the Lord reveals Himself to the slave girl, Hagar, as **"the God who sees"** spoken in Hebrew as "**El Roiy:**"

The Lord reveals Himself to Israel as **"Jehovah Rapha** "which means **"The Lord Who Heals You."** We read about this in Exodus 15:26.

After the victory in the war between the Israelites and the Amalekites, the revelation for Moses and Israel is the following: We see Moses erecting an altar to God, declaring with it **"Jehovah Nissi"** meaning "The **Lord My Banner/the Lord my Victory** " Read about this in Exodus 17:15.

Gideon experiences several revelations from the Lord during his divine encounter and command in which he is told to fight against the Midianites. On one such occasion he erects an altar to the Lord, offering to the Lord, declaring that the Lord is **"Jehovah Shalom" which** means **"the Lord is Peace."** Shalom means more than we normally connect to peace. Peace in Hebrew perspective also includes prosperity, health, success, and many more blessings. Gideon also learned here that God thought more of him as he thought of himself, as God had deposited potential in him, that he still needed to discover. His power was established in the Lord, and by putting his trust in God, he would overcome and enjoy peace.

In 1 Samuel 1:3, the Lord is defined as **"Jehovah Sabaoth,** "meaning "**the Lord of hosts — the Almighty."**

David's experience of love and faith in the Lord leads him on the path of various revelations about the Lord he serves. At Psalm 7:18, he describes the Lord as **"Jehovah Elyon" meaning** the "**Most High God."** In Psalm 23, David defines the Lord as **"Jehovah Raah"** — **"the Lord is my Shepherd."**

In Jeremiah 23:6, Jeremiah prophesies about the coming of Jesus and says in verse 6"... and it is **His Name with which He will be called "Jehovah Tsidkenu,"** which means **"Jehovah My Righteousness."**

Ezekiel 48:34 prophetically states: **"Jehovah Shammah"** means "**Jehovah Is There/... is here."**

There is so much to be said about the revelation of God in the Old Testament, including...
"Jehovah M'kadesh" meaning "**Lord My Sanctifier**" in Exodus 31:13; and
"El Olam" – **"Everlasting God"** as defined in Genesis 21:33.

One of the wonders of the **Old Testament is that it is a shadow of the New Testament**, for example, it is constantly finger-pointing to Jesus' coming as a human being, yet God, in the New Testament. Please read Hebrews 8:5-7,10-13, and Hebrews 10:1.

One of the most outstanding prophetic words is that of **Isaiah 9:6: "For unto us a child is born, unto us a Son is given; And the dominion (government) is upon His shoulder, and He is called Wonderful, Counselor, Mighty God, Everlasting Father, Prince of Peace,"**

Isaiah is known as the Messianic prophet since the Lord used him to foretell Jesus ' coming so much. This prediction of Jesus' coming is a powerful revelation of Jesus' characteristics and authority.

There is much more that reveals God's character in the Old Testament, but let's see what we find when we enter the **New Testament**... This is where we discover the greatness of our Heavenly Father as we hear Jesus' statements that are accurately aligned with God Himself.

In Matthew 1:18,20, we see how **Jesus— God who became man— was begotten by the Holy Spirit in Mary.** In a dream, Joseph is informed about this by an angel of the Lord. Joseph is said to call this son **"Jesus" which means "it is He who will save His people from their sins."** In verses 22-23, we see the prophecy of Isaiah 7:14 being fulfilled while another name of Jesus which reveals His character is mentioned. This passage says: "... And they shall call **His Name Immanuel, which is translated, <u>God with us."</u>**

God the Father Himself, confirms who Jesus is by declaring Him to be the Son of God. See Matthew 3:17.

In Matthew 4:17, Jesus identifies Himself as a **"Bearer and Representative" of the Kingdom of Heaven when He says: "Repent, for the <u>kingdom of heaven is near/the kingdom of heaven is at hand.</u>"** In fact, **Jesus is the embodiment of the Kingdom of God while He is all that the Heavenly Kingdom of God entails.**

Jesus begins to declare and reveal Himself as God through what He says to the people. He explains His real origin in John 7:29 by saying that **He is from God Himself and sent by God.**

In John 8:12 and John 9:5, Jesus states: **"I am the Light of the world; He who follows Me will not walk in darkness but will have the light of life."**

Notice how **Jesus begins with "I AM..."** which aligns **with God's identity** in essence when He said to Moses: **"I AM, WHAT I AM"** in Hebrew **"YHWH,"** as defined in Exodus 3:14.

In John 6:48, Jesus says, **"I am the Bread of Life,** "while God fed Israel with manna from heaven, the surpassing comparison comes that **Jesus Himself is the spiritual bread of eternal value that nourishes our spirit.**

Jesus also offers us the living water of **His Word and Spirit**. **This type of water is the living waters that He alone can give** as defined in John 7:37-39.

In John 10:10, Jesus says, **"I am the door,"** and in verse 11 He says, **"I am the good Shepherd..."** This latter statement is in line with David's experience of God in Psalm 23.

We see further in John 11:25 how Jesus declares: **"I am the Resurrection and the Life, whoever believes in Me, will live even if he dies."** What a wonderful hope we have in Jesus Christ!

Jesus also states in John 14:6: **"I am the Way, the Truth, and the Life; no one comes to the Father except through Me." Jesus is the only way to true life. No other God can bring us out of there.**

Jesus promises us revelation of Himself and His Father, if we truly love Him and keep (abide/obey) His will and commandments. It is defined in John 14:20,21,23. Jesus further reinforces this fact in John 15:5 when He says: **"I am the vine, you are the branches. He that**

abides in Me, and I in him, he bears much fruit; For apart from Me you can do nothing. " The evidence of WHO has taken residence in us, is to be found in the fruit we bear.

In Colossians 2:9, Paul says, **"For in Him dwells the fullness of the Godhead physically..."** So, Jesus has the divine nature in Him and acted accordingly on earth.

There are many more explanations in the Bible that reveals Jesus as God. One of the important verses in this regard is found in **1 John 5:20 "And we know that the Son of God has come and has given us understanding to know Him who is <u>true;</u> And we are in Him that is true, in His Son, <u>Jesus Christ</u>. He is the true God and eternal life."**

For John, Jesus is **also synonymous with Perfect, Upright, True, Eternal LOVE**... as defined in 1 John 4:7-9, 16-18.

Finally, but not least, regarding the Biblical explanations of who Jesus is, we look at Revelation where Jesus says: **"I am the Alpha and the Omega, the first and the last...** "Furthermore, in verses 17-18, Jesus **declares that He is alive; He was dead, but now he lives forever. He has the keys of Hades and of Death.** We see Jesus **as the Lamb of God** in Revelation 5, as well as the **"Lion of Judah"** in Verse 5; **as the Bridegroom** in Revelation 19 and in verse 11 we see **Him on a white horse:** "Then I saw heaven opened; And there was a white horse, and **He that sat on it was called <u>Faithful and True</u>, and He judges and makes war in righteousness."** In verse 13, we see that **His Name is also "<u>the Word of God</u>."**

In Revelation 19:10b and verse 16 Jesus is identified as the **"<u>Spirit of Prophecy</u>"** and as the **"<u>King of kings and the Lord of lords</u>."** There is most certainly no greater God than He!!

"Now <u>unto the King</u> Eternal, Immortal, Invisible, <u>the Only Wise God</u>, be honor and glory for ever and ever.
Amen."
1 Timothy 1:17

HOW DO I SEE AND EXPERIENCE GOD PERSONALLY?

The answer to this question lies in your personal experience and relationship with Jesus Christ.

I know God as:
- The Center of my existence,
- The God who makes the impossible possible,
- That pours His love out on me in abundance, unconditionally,
- The God who shows me His goodness, mercy, and grace continually,
- And just as He holds the universe in the hollow of His hand, likewise, He also holds me in His mighty loving hand.
- My great Physician of spirit, soul, and body,
- My Leader, Redeemer, Provider and True Friend,
- An intimate, personal God who is intensely interested in you and me, so intensely that our names are engraved in the palm of His hand, so that He continually thinks of us...

> *BUT...*

When I think of my First True Love, Jesus, in my life, my heart overflows with a deep admiration, which I experience as follows:

God is in the fresh morning breeze touching my face at dawn, playfully blowing softly around me, to announce His presence...

God is in every dewdrop that shines like diamonds in the morning sun's rays.

He is in every blossom that slowly folds open to show its beauty to the world. In every flower's fragrance, I find another facet of His glorious presence.

God is also in the drops of rain, stirring up the barren earth to new life, for He is the Source of all life!

And in every fresh stream of water, flowing through the mountains, yes, even in the ramblings of thunder, I hear His voice...

The clouds are the dust of His feet and the sun's rays, a reflection of His eternal glory...

When I look up at the mountains, I am amazed amid the power and authority He reveals in them.

As I walk through a rainforest, I stand in awe at the sight of His artwork unfolding in every plant, flower, tree, moss covered rock and shrub...

When I see the sea stretched out before me in all its greatness and splendor, echoing its noise in my ears, I can't help but be overwhelmed by His majesty and glory!

In the morning, when the birds joyfully bring their praises to their Creator, it also fills my heart with a grateful song of praise to Him who makes every day new...

When I see the eagle in its flight, or see a buck peacefully move between the shrubs at a stream of water, or even see the cheetah running across the field at full speed, it fills my heart with deep wonder and awe at the incredible creativity my Creator reveals in this.

Yes, even so, He is the refreshing living waters, which He pours out within me, to refresh my spirit and soul, but also to equip me for service to others, for His Name's sake...

When seeing a newborn baby, I can't help but experience the purity of true life, as God intended it to be...

In every excited child voice, in every child's laughter, I hear Jesus' words saying to me anew: "Unless you become like this little child, you will not see the kingdom of God..."
When I become aware of the absolute trust and perfect, sincere faith of a child, I realize anew the wonder of true faith in an everlasting Abba Father...

When a true, sincere, God-given friend crosses the path of my life, and I taste the fullness of true friendship, I once again become aware of Jesus as my Perfect Friend. The Friend with whom I can even pour out my deepest longings and heart's desires and I know He understands...

And when life comes to knock me down, I feel my God's mighty hand under me, ready to heal my brokenness once again, to re-establish my spirit, and to set my feet on victory ground.

He is my Comforter who brings my turbulent heart back to calmness, peace, and order. My Abba Father who wraps His arms around me, when I yearn for His comforting nearness or just want to sit at His feet to learn from Him...

He is the God who pours out grace, mercy, and forgiveness on me when I fail in weakness to do His will. Yes, it is He who loves me so much that He lets His Son die on the cross, when I deserved it!

It is God who even planned your and my birth and wrote a divine hopeful future plan in His book of life for us.

God is the One who breaks the brass chains of evil, who opens and closes doors that no one can close or open again. When He frees us, we are truly free!

He is as near to me as my shadow on my right hand and at the same time He holds my hand to guide me through life...

With every unconscious, automatic breath I take and every heartbeat that beats so softly inside me, I experience His life-giving power that sustains me.

Yet He is high and exalted, holy, and wonderful!

As I approach His throne of grace in my spirit, there is no greater honor than to fall at His feet and cry out with the elders and angels: **"Holy, holy, holy is the Lord God Almighty! He who was and is and always will be! Holy is His Name!"**

I want to close by witnessing with John that if we were to describe EVERYTHING about the Lord, and what Jesus did during His walk on earth, the world would not be big enough to contain all the written books!

".... They never rest day or night, saying:
"Holy, Holy, Holy is the Lord God, the All-Powerful,
Who was and who is, and who is still to come!"

"You are worthy, our Lord and God,
to receive glory and honor and power,
since you created all things,
and because of Your will they existed and were created!"
Revelation 4:8b & 11

All glory to our Abba Father and Lord throughout all the centuries to come!

AMEN.

REFERENCES

- The Bible – Different Translations
- The Word and E-Sword software programs
- Many Voices One Message – Pastor Bert Murray
- Die Hoogste Roeping – Pastor Bert Murray
- Science of the heart; Exploring the role of the heart in human performance; chapter 1, Heart-Brain communication – Heart Math Institute
- Becoming a Vessel of Honor - Rebecca Brown
- Think Learn Succeed - Dr Caroline Leaf
- The Perfect You – Dr Caroline Leaf
- Die kind van die krip is my God – Pastor Bert Murray
- The Oneness of God – David K Bernard
- Apostolic Formation: www.apostolicformation.com & info@apostolicformation.com
  Visit the website and enjoy further in-depth life-changing Bible studies.

ALL ABOUT THE AUTHOR

Sharon Elizabeth De Jager is the youngest of three children. Her parents were from childhood, a great inspiration to the enduring spiritual interest in her life. Her parents were not only active in church activities, but regularly held family worship & prayer sessions that laid a strong foundation in her life.

At the age of 12, she surrendered her life to the Lord, which brought about the beginning of her growing, intimate, lifelong relationship with Abba Father. Her constant hunger for the Word of God motivated her to learn more and more about her Heavenly King, Father, and Savior. Her in-depth study of Scripture led her to spiritual revelations and the discovery of deeper meanings and messages behind the obvious black letters of the Bible.

In 1982, she obtained a Diploma in General Nursing and Midwifery at SG Lourens College in Pretoria, South Africa, followed, by a Certificate in Genetics, at the Department of National Health and later studied counselling through Turning Point Counselling Network, where she obtained internationally recognized certificates in Deep Level Emotional Therapy and Child Counselling.

She was ordained pastor at Salem Family Church in 2014.

She was involved in the nursing profession for 42 years full-time and retired in February 2021. During her interactions with patients, she not only noticed their physical illness, but also their mental and emotional needs, which she addressed when the opportunity was there and the patient desired assistance.

Her interest in counselling began with the awareness of the need in a congregation's children's church where the brokenness of the children, was identified with anonymous children's prayer requests. There was no facilitator in this congregation who could effectively deal with these childhood problems. During her counseling studies, she realized that she herself also needed inner healing, due to a traumatic divorce and brokenness of the past. She walked, the path of healing with the Lord and a counselor and received the precious, heavenly gift of inner healing. It is out of gratitude for what God has done in her life, that she helps others on the path of inner healing, with God's Word, the Bible as the guide.

Her love of writing has evolved from in her teens, born from a feeling that she can better express herself on paper, communicate with her Heavenly Father in this way as well, and make others aware of God as a loving Father who is intensely interested in humankind and who is still relevant today. At the same time, she could convey that the true Answer to the World's Problems and True Happiness, is to be found in Jesus. Her writings are also the product of her own spiritual growth and experiences with the Lord. The writings also depict her spiritual journey of discovery. Among other things, she discovered that there is hope and life after a traumatic divorce, especially if you take refuge in Abba Father and allow Him to be your Comforter, Counselor, Prince of Peace and Savior.

She is currently happily married to a man who, she is convinced, was chosen for her by her heavenly Father and is also the mother of two adopted children and one biological child. They live in Pretoria, South Africa.

This book is the result of a Spirit driven urgency in her heart to make other people aware of God as a wonderful true Reality, which could be discovered between the pages of the spiritual pearls which she gathered along life's path as God revealed His spiritual treasures and secrets unto her. These spiritual pearls simultaneously reveal answers to the many spiritual questions people might have who are seeking a more intimate relationship with God. It is an opportunity to collect many spiritual treasures which will serve as blessings in your life.

Her vision is far beyond the horizon of this world, aimed at the heavenly destination, where one day she will meet her Lord and Master face to face — in keeping with the Scriptures: "Therefore, since we are surrounded by such a great cloud of witnesses, we must get rid of every weight and the sin that clings so closely and **run with endurance the race set out for us, keeping our eyes fixed on Jesus, the Pioneer and Perfecter of our faith. ...**" Hebrews 12:1b,2.

****

www.ingramcontent.com/pod-product-compliance
Lightning Source LLC
Chambersburg PA
CBHW071403120626
46546CB00002B/794